KNOWLEDGE OF THE
HIGHER WORLDS
AND ITS ATTAINMENT

by
RUDOLF STEINER

ANTHROPOSOPHIC PRESS, INC.

BELL'S POND

HUDSON, NEW YORK

This volume is a translation of *Wie erlangt man Erkenntnisse der höheren Welten?* (Vol. 10 in the Bibliographic Survey, 1961). It was rendered into English by George Metaxa with revisions by Henry B. and Lisa D. Monges.

Cover Design Motif: Rudolf Steiner
Lettering: Peter Stebbing

Printed in the United States of America

CONTENTS

Preface to the Third Edition

Herewith appear in book form my expositions originally published as single essays under the title *Knowledge of the Higher Worlds and Its Attainment*. For the present, this volume offers the first part; one that is to follow will constitute the continuation. This work on a development of man that will enable him to grasp the supersensible worlds cannot be presented to the public in a new form without certain comments which I shall now make. The communications it contains concerning the development of the human soul are intended to fill various needs.

First of all, something is to be offered those people who feel drawn to the results of spiritual research, and who must raise the question: "Well, whence do those persons derive their knowledge who claim the ability to tell us something of the profound riddles of life?"—Spiritual science does this. Whoever wishes to observe the facts leading to such claims must rise to supersensible cognition. He must follow the path I have endeavored to describe in this book. On the other hand, it would be an error to imagine these disclosures of spiritual science to be valueless for one who lacks the inclination or the possibility to pursue this path himself. In order to establish the facts through research, the ability to enter the supersensible worlds is indispensable; but once they have been discovered and communicated, even one who does not perceive them himself can be adequately convinced of their truth. A large proportion of them can be tested offhand, simply by applying ordinary common sense in a genuinely unprejudiced way. Only, one must not let this open-mindedness become confused by any of the pre-conceived ideas so common in human life. Someone can easily believe, for example, that some statement or other contradicts certain facts established by modern science. In reality, there is no such thing as a scientific fact that contradicts spiritual science; but there can easily seem to be contradictions unless scientific conclusions are consulted abundantly and without prejudice. The student will find that the more open-mindedly he compares spiritual science with positive scientific achievements, the more clearly is complete accord to be seen.

Another category of spiritual-scientific disclosures, it is true, will be found to elude purely mental judgment more or less; but the right relation to these also will be achieved without great difficulty by one who understands that not the mind alone but healthy feeling as well is qualified to determine what is true. And when this feeling does not permit itself to be warped by a liking or antipathy for some opinion or other, but really allows higher knowledge to act without prejudice, a corresponding sentient judgment results.

And there are many more ways of confirming this knowledge for those who cannot or do not wish to tread the path into the supersensible world. Such people can feel very clearly what value this knowledge has in life, even when it comes to them only through the communications of those engaged in spiritual research. Not everyone can immediately achieve spiritual vision; but the discoveries of those who have it can be health-giving life-nourishment for all. For everyone can apply them; and whoever does so will soon discover what life in every branch can be with their aid, and what it lacks without them. The results of supersensible knowledge, when properly employed in life, prove to be—not unpractical, but rather, practical in the highest sense.

One who does not himself intend to follow the path to higher knowledge, but is interested in the facts it reveals, can ask: How does the seer arrive at these facts? To such a one this book is intended to picture the path in such a way that even one not following it can nevertheless have confidence in the communications of the person who has done so. Realizing how the spiritual scientist works, he can approve, and say to himself: The impression made upon me by the description of this path to the higher worlds makes clear why the facts reported seem reasonable. Thus this book is intended to help those who want their sense of truth and feeling for truth concerning the supersensible world strengthened and assured.

No less, however, does it aim to offer aid to those who themselves seek the way to supersensible knowledge. The truth of what is here set forth will best be verified by those who achieve its reality within themselves. Anyone with this intention will do well to keep reminding himself that in an exposition on the development of the soul, more is called for than becoming acquainted with the substance, which is frequently the aim in other expositions. It is necessary to familiarize oneself intimately with the presentation. One must postulate the following: no single matter is to be comprehended only by means of what is said about the matter itself, but by means of much else that is disclosed concerning totally different matters. This will develop the conception that what is vital is to be found not in any single truth but in the harmony of all truths. This must be seriously considered by anyone intending to carry out the exercises. An exercise can be rightly understood and even rightly executed, and yet produce a wrong effect unless another be added to it—one that will resolve the one-sidedness of the first into a harmony of the soul. Whoever reads this book in an intimate way, so that the reading resembles an inner experience, will not merely familiarize himself with its contents: one passage will evoke a certain feeling, another passage another feeling;

and in that way he will learn how much importance should be seen in the one or the other in the development of his soul. He will also find out in what form he should try this or that exercise, what form best suits his particular individuality. When one has to do, as is the case here, with descriptions of processes that are to be *experienced,* it is necessary to refer again and again to the content; for it will become manifest that much can be satisfactorily assimilated only after trial, which in turn reveals certain finer points that at first are bound to be overlooked.

Even those readers who do not intend to take the way prescribed will find much in the book that can be of service to the inner life, such as maxims, suggestions that throw light on various puzzling problems, and so on.

And those who have had experiences in their lives that serve, to some extent, as an initiation through life may derive a certain satisfaction from finding clarified through co-ordination what had haunted them as separate problems—things they already knew, but perhaps without having been able to consolidate them in adequate conceptions.

x

Preface to the Fifth Edition

In preparing this new edition of *Knowledge of the Higher Worlds and Its Attainment* I have gone over every detail of the subject as I had presented it over ten years ago. The urge to make such a review is natural in the case of disclosures concerning soul experiences and paths such as are indicated in this book. There can be no portion of what is imparted which does not remain intimately a part of the one who communicates it, or which does not contain something that perpetually works upon his soul. And it is inevitable that this work of the soul should be joined by an endeavor to enhance the clarity and lucidity of the presentation as given years before. This engendered what I have endeavored to accomplish in this new edition. All the essential elements of the expositions, all the principal points, have remained as they were; yet important changes have been made. In many passages I have been able to increase the accuracy of characterization in detail, and this seemed to me important. If anyone wishes to apply what is imparted in this book to his own spiritual life, it is important that he should be able to contemplate the paths in question by means of a characterization as exact as possible. Misconceptions can arise in far greater measure in connection with the description of inner spiritual processes than with that of facts in the physical world. The mobility of the soul life, the danger of losing sight of how different it is from all life in the physical world—this and much else renders such misunderstandings possible. In preparing this new edition I have directed my attention to finding passages in which misconceptions might arise, and I have endeavored to forestall them.

At the time I wrote the essays that constitute this book, much had to be discussed in a different way from today, because at that time I had to allude in a different manner to the substance of what has been published since then concerning facts of cognition of spiritual worlds. In my *Occult*

Science, in *The Spiritual Guidance of Mankind,* in *A Road to Self-Knowledge and the Threshold of the Spiritual World,* as well as in other writings, spiritual processes are described whose existence, to be sure, was already inevitably indicated in this book ten years ago, but in words differing from those that seem right today. In connection with a great deal not described in the book I had to explain at that time that it could be learned by oral communication. Much of what this referred to has since been published. But these allusions perhaps did not wholly exclude the possibility of erroneous ideas in the reader's mind. It might be possible, for instance, to imagine something much more vital in the personal relations between the seeker for spiritual schooling and this or that teacher than is intended. I trust I have here succeeded, by presenting details in a certain way, in emphasizing more strongly that for one seeking spiritual schooling in accord with present spiritual conditions an absolutely direct relation to the objective spiritual world is of far greater importance than a relation to the personality of a teacher. The latter will gradually become merely the helper; he will assume the same position in spiritual schooling as a teacher occupies, in conformity with modern views, in any other field of knowledge. I believe I have sufficiently stressed the fact that the teacher's authority and the pupil's faith in him should play no greater part in spiritual schooling than in any other branch of knowledge or life. A great deal depends, it seems to me, upon an increasingly true estimate of this relation between the one who carries on spiritual research and those who develop an interest in the results of his research. Thus I believe I have improved the book wherever I was in a position, after ten years, to find what needs improving.

A second part is to be added to this first part, bringing further explanations of the frame of mind that can lead a man to the experience of the higher worlds.

The new edition of the book, the printing completed, lay before me when the great war now being experienced by mankind broke out. I must write these prefatory remarks while my soul is deeply moved by the destiny-laden event.

Rudolf Steiner

Berlin, September 7, 1914.

Preface to the Edition of May 1918

In working over this new edition I found only minor changes in its substance necessary; but I have added an appendix in which I have endeavored to explain more clearly the psychological foundations to which the disclosures contained in the book must be traced if they are to be accepted without risk of misunderstanding. I believe that the contents of the appendix will also serve to show many an opponent of anthroposophical spiritual science that his judgment is based upon a misconception of the nature of this spiritual science; that he does not see what it really is.

Rudolf Steiner

I

HOW IS KNOWLEDGE OF THE HIGHER WORLDS ATTAINED?

Conditions

THERE slumber in every human being faculties by means of which he can acquire for himself a knowledge of higher worlds. Mystics, Gnostics, Theosophists—all speak of a world of soul and spirit which for them is just as real as the world we see with our physical eyes and touch with our physical hands. At every moment the listener may say to himself: that, of which they speak, I too can learn, if I develop within myself certain powers which today still slumber within me. There remains only one question— how to set to work to develop such faculties. For this purpose, they only can give advice who already possess such powers. As long as the human race has existed there has always been a method of training, in the course of which individuals possessing these higher faculties gave instruction to others who were in search of them. Such a training is called occult (esoteric) training, and the instruction received therefrom is called occult (esoteric) teaching, or spiritual science. This designation naturally awakens misunderstanding. The one who hears it may very easily be misled into the belief that this training is the concern of a special, privileged class, withholding its knowledge arbitrarily from its fellow-creatures. He may even think that nothing of real importance lies behind such knowledge, for if it were a true knowledge—he is tempted to think—there would be no need of making a secret of it; it might be publicly imparted and its advantages made accessible to all. Those who have been initiated into the nature of this higher knowledge are not in the least surprised that the uninitiated should so think, for the secret of initiation can only be understood by those who have to a certain degree experienced this initiation into the higher knowledge of existence. The question may be raised: how, then, under these circumstances, are the uninitiated to develop any human interest in this so-called esoteric knowl-

2

edge? How and why are they to seek for something of whose nature they can form no idea? Such a question is based upon an entirely erroneous conception of the real nature of esoteric knowledge. There is, in truth, no difference between esoteric knowledge and all the rest of man's knowledge and proficiency. This esoteric knowledge is no more of a secret for the average human being than writing is a secret for those who have never learned it. And just as all can learn to write who choose the correct method, so, too, can all who seek the right way become esoteric students and even teachers. In one respect only do the conditions here differ from those that apply to external knowledge and proficiency. The possibility of acquiring the art of writing may be withheld from someone through poverty, or through the conditions of civilization into which he is born; but for the attainment of knowledge and proficiency in the higher worlds, there is no obstacle for those who earnestly seek them.

Many believe that they must seek, at one place or another, the masters of higher knowledge in order to receive enlightenment. Now in the first place, whoever strives earnestly after higher

3

knowledge will shun no exertion and fear no obstacle in his search for an initiate who can lead him to the higher knowledge of the world. On the other hand, everyone may be certain that initiation will find him under all circumstances if he gives proof of an earnest and worthy endeavor to attain this knowledge. It is a natural law among all initiates to withhold from no man the knowledge that is due him; but there is an equally natural law which lays down that no word of esoteric knowledge shall be imparted to anyone not qualified to receive it. And the more strictly he observes these laws, the more perfect is an initiate. The bond of union embracing all initiates is spiritual and not external, but the two laws here mentioned form, as it were, strong clasps by which the component parts of this bond are held together. You may live in intimate friendship with an initiate, and yet a gap severs you from his essential self, so long as you have not become an initiate yourself. You may enjoy in the fullest sense the heart, the love of an initiate, yet he will only confide his knowledge to you when you are ripe for it. You may flatter him; you may torture him; nothing can induce him to betray anything

4

to you as long as you, at the present stage of your evolution, are not competent to receive it into your soul in the right way.

The methods by which a student is prepared for the reception of higher knowledge are minutely prescribed. The direction he is to take is traced with unfading, everlasting letters in the worlds of the spirit where the initiates guard the higher secrets. In ancient times, anterior to our history, the temples of the spirit were also outwardly visible; today, because our life has become so unspiritual, they are not to be found in the world visible to external sight; yet they are present spiritually everywhere, and all who seek may find them.

Only within his own soul can a man find the means to unseal the lips of an initiate. He must develop within himself certain faculties to a definite degree, and then the highest treasures of the spirit can become his own.

He must begin with a certain fundamental attitude of soul. In spiritual science this fundamental attitude is called the *path of veneration,* of devotion to truth and knowledge. Without this attitude no one can become a student. The dis-

5

position shown in their childhood by subsequent students of higher knowledge is well known to the experienced in these matters. There are children who look up with religious awe to those whom they venerate. For such people they have a respect which forbids them, even in the deepest recess of their heart, to harbor any thought of criticism or opposition. Such children grow up into young men and women who feel happy when they are able to look up to anything that fills them with veneration. From the ranks of such children are recruited many students of higher knowledge. Have you ever paused outside the door of some venerated person, and have you, on this your first visit, felt a religious awe as you pressed on the handle to enter the room which for you is a holy place? If so, a feeling has been manifested within you which may be the germ of your future adherence to the path of knowledge. It is a blessing for every human being in process of development to have such feelings upon which to build. Only it must not be thought that this disposition leads to submissiveness and slavery. What was once a childlike veneration for persons becomes, later, a veneration for truth and knowl-

6

edge. Experience teaches that they can best hold their heads erect who have learnt to venerate where veneration is due; and veneration is always fitting when it flows from the depths of the heart.

If we do not develop within ourselves this deeply rooted feeling that there is something higher than ourselves, we shall never find the strength to evolve to something higher. The initiate has only acquired the strength to lift his head to the heights of knowledge by guiding his heart to the depths of veneration and devotion. The heights of the spirit can only be climbed by passing through the portals of humility. You can only acquire right knowledge when you have learnt to esteem it. Man has certainly the right to turn his eyes to the light, but he must first acquire this right. There are laws in the spiritual life, as in the physical life. Rub a glass rod with an appropriate material and it will become electric, that is, it will receive the power of attracting small bodies. This is in keeping with a law of nature. It is known to all who have learnt a little physics. Similarly, acquaintance with the first principles of spiritual science shows that every feeling of true devotion harbored in the soul develops a power which may, sooner or later, lead further on the path of knowledge.

The student who is gifted with this feeling, or who is fortunate enough to have had it inculcated in a suitable education, brings a great deal along with him when, later in life, he seeks admittance to higher knowledge. Failing such preparation, he will encounter difficulties at the very first step, unless he undertakes, by rigorous self-education, to create within himself this inner life of devotion. In our time it is especially important that full attention be paid to this point. Our civilization tends more toward critical judgment and condemnation than toward devotion and selfless veneration. Our children already criticize far more than they worship. But every criticism, every adverse judgment passed, disperses the powers of the soul for the attainment of higher knowledge, in the same measure that all veneration and reverence develops them. In this we do not wish to say anything against our civilization. There is no question here of leveling criticism against it. To this critical faculty, this self-conscious human judgment, this "test all things and

8

hold fast what is best," we owe the greatness of our civilization. Man could never have attained to the science, the industry, the commerce, the rights relationships of our time, had he not applied to all things the standard of his critical judgment. But what we have thereby gained in external culture we have had to pay for with a corresponding loss of higher knowledge of spiritual life. It must be emphasized that higher knowledge is not concerned with the veneration of persons but the veneration of truth and knowledge.

Now, the one thing that everyone must acknowledge is the difficulty for those involved in the external civilization of our time to advance to the knowledge of the higher worlds. They can only do so if they work energetically at themselves. At a time when the conditions of material life were simpler, the attainment of spiritual knowledge was also easier. Objects of veneration and worship stood out in clearer relief from the ordinary things of the world. In an epoch of criticism ideals are lowered; other feelings take the place of veneration, respect, adoration, and wonder. Our own age thrusts these feelings further and further into the background, so that they can only be conveyed to man through his every-day life in a very small degree. Whoever seeks higher knowledge must create it for himself. He must instil it into his soul. It cannot be done by study; it can only be done through life. Whoever, therefore, wishes to become a student of higher knowledge must assiduously cultivate this inner life of devotion. Everywhere in his environment and his experiences he must seek motives of admiration and homage. If I meet a man and blame him for his shortcomings, I rob myself of power to attain higher knowledge; but if I try to enter lovingly into his merits, I gather such power. The student must continually be intent upon following this advice. The spiritually experienced know how much they owe to the circumstance that in face of all things they ever again turn to the good, and withhold adverse judgment. But this must not remain an external rule of life; rather it must take possession of our innermost soul. Man has it in his power to perfect himself and, in time, completely to transform himself. But this transformation must take place in his innermost self, in his thought-life. It is not enough that I show respect only in my outward bearing; I must have this respect in my thoughts. The student must begin by absorbing this devotion into his thought-life. He must be wary of thoughts of disrespect, of adverse criticism, existing in his consciousness, and he must endeavor straightaway to cultivate thoughts of devotion.

Every moment that we set ourselves to discover in our consciousness whatever there remains in it of adverse, disparaging and critical judgment of the world and of life; every such moment brings us nearer to higher knowledge. And we rise rapidly when we fill our consciousness in such moments with thoughts evoking in us admiration, respect, and veneration for the world and for life. It is well known to those experienced in these matters that in every such moment powers are awakened which otherwise remain dormant. In this way the spiritual eyes of man are opened. He begins to see things around him which he could not have seen before. He begins to understand that hitherto he had only seen a part of the world around him. A human being standing before him now presents a new and different aspect. Of course, this rule of life alone will not yet enable him to see, for instance, what is described as the human aura, because for this still higher training is necessary. But he can rise to this higher training if he has previously undergone a rigorous training in devotion. (In the last chapter of his book *Theosophy,* the author describes fully the *Path of Knowledge;* here it is intended to give some practical details.)

Noiseless and unnoticed by the outer world is the treading of the *Path of Knowledge.* No change need be noticed in the student. He performs his duties as hitherto; he attends to his business as before. The transformation goes on only in the inner part of the soul hidden from outward sight. At first his entire inner life is flooded by this basic feeling of devotion for everything which is truly venerable. His entire soul-life finds in this fundamental feeling its pivot. Just as the sun's rays vivify everything living, so does reverence in the student vivify all feelings of the soul.

It is not easy, at first, to believe that feelings like reverence and respect have anything to do with cognition. This is due to the fact that we are inclined to set cognition aside as a faculty by itself—one that stands in no relation to what otherwise occurs in the soul. In so thinking we do not bear in mind that it is the soul which exercises the faculty of cognition; and feelings are for the soul what food is for the body. If we give the body stones in place of bread, its activity will cease. It is the same with the soul. Veneration, homage, devotion are like nutriment making it healthy and strong, especially strong for the activity of cognition. Disrespect, antipathy, underestimation of what deserves recognition, all exert a paralyzing and withering effect on this faculty of cognition. For the spiritually experienced this fact is visible in the aura. A soul which harbors feelings of reverence and devotion produces a change in its aura. Certain spiritual colorings, as they may be called, yellow-red and brown-red in tone, vanish and are replaced by blue-red tints. Thereby the cognitional faculty is ripened; it receives intelligence of facts in its environment of which it had hitherto no idea. Reverence awakens in the soul a sympa-

13

thetic power through which we attract qualities in the beings around us, which would otherwise remain concealed.

The power obtained through devotion can be rendered still more effective when the life of feeling is enriched by yet another quality. This consists in giving oneself up less and less to impressions of the outer world, and to develop instead a vivid inner life. A person who darts from one impression of the outer world to another, who constantly seeks distraction, cannot find the way to higher knowledge. The student must not blunt himself to the outer world, but while lending himself to its impressions, he should be directed by his rich inner life. When passing through a beautiful mountain district, the traveller with depth of soul and wealth of feeling has different experiences from one who is poor in feeling. Only what we experience within ourselves unlocks for us the beauties of the outer world. One person sails across the ocean, and only a few inward experiences pass through his soul; another will hear the eternal language of the cosmic spirit; for him are unveiled the mysterious riddles of existence. We must learn to remain in

14

touch with our own feelings and ideas if we wish to develop any intimate relationship with the outer world. The outer world with all its phenomena is filled with divine splendor, but we must have experienced the divine within ourselves before we can hope to discover it in our environment.

The student is told to set apart moments in his daily life in which to withdraw into himself, quietly and alone. He is not to occupy himself at such moments with the affairs of his own ego. This would result in the contrary of what is intended. He should rather let his experiences and the messages from the outer world re-echo within his own completely silent self. At such silent moments every flower, every animal, every action will unveil to him secrets undreamt of. And thus he will prepare himself to receive quite new impressions of the outer world through quite different eyes. The desire to enjoy impression after impression merely blunts the faculty of cognition; the latter, however, is nurtured and cultivated if the enjoyment once experienced is allowed to reveal its message. Thus the student must accustom himself not merely to let the enjoyment reverberate, as it were, but rather to renounce any further enjoyment, and work upon the past experience. The peril here is very great. Instead of working inwardly, it is very easy to fall into the opposite habit of trying to exploit the enjoyment. Let no one underestimate the fact that immense sources of error here confront the student. He must pass through a host of tempters of his soul. They would all harden his ego and imprison it within itself. He should rather open it wide to all the world. It is necessary that he should seek enjoyment, for only through enjoyment can the outer world reach him. If he blunts himself to enjoyment he is like a plant which cannot any longer draw nourishment from its environment. Yet if he stops short at the enjoyment he shuts himself up within himself. He will only be something to himself and nothing to the world. However much he may live within himself, however intensely he may cultivate his ego —the world will reject him. To the world he is dead. The student of higher knowledge considers enjoyment only as a means of ennobling himself for the world. Enjoyment is to him like a scout informing him about the world; but once instructed by enjoyment, he passes on to work. He does not learn in order to accumulate learning as his own treasure, but in order that he may devote his learning to the service of the world.

In all spiritual science there is a fundamental principle which cannot be transgressed without sacrificing success, and it should be impressed on the student in every form of esoteric training. It runs as follows: *All knowledge pursued merely for the enrichment of personal learning and the accumulation of personal treasure leads you away from the path; but all knowledge pursued for growth to ripeness within the process of human ennoblement and cosmic development brings you a step forward.* This law must be strictly observed, and no student is genuine until he has adopted it as a guide for his whole life. This truth can be expressed in the following short sentence: *Every idea which does not become your ideal slays a force in your soul; every idea which becomes your ideal creates within you life-forces.*

Inner Tranquillity

At the very beginning of his course, the student is directed to the path of veneration and the development of the inner life. Spiritual science now also gives him practical rules by observing which he may tread that path and develop that inner life. These practical rules have no arbitrary origin. They rest upon ancient experience and ancient wisdom, and are given out in the same manner, wheresoever the ways to higher knowledge are indicated. All true teachers of the spiritual life are in agreement as to the substance of these rules, even though they do not always clothe them in the same words. This difference, which is of a minor character and is more apparent than real, is due to circumstances which need not be dwelt upon here.

No teacher of the spiritual life wishes to establish a mastery over other persons by means of such rules. He would not tamper with anyone's independence. Indeed, none respect and cherish human independence more than the spiritually experienced. It was stated in the preceding pages that the bond of union embracing all initiates is spiritual, and that two laws form, as it were, clasps by which the component parts of this bond are held together. Whenever the initiate leaves his enclosed spiritual sphere and steps forth before the world, he must immediately take a third law into account. It is this: Adapt each one of your actions, and frame each one of your words in such a way that you infringe upon no one's free-will.

The recognition that all true teachers of the spiritual life are permeated through and through with this principle will convince all who follow the practical rules proffered to them that they need sacrifice none of their independence.

One of the first of these rules can be expressed somewhat in the following words of our language: *Provide for yourself moments of inner tranquillity, and in these moments learn to distinguish between the essential and the none-essential.* It is said advisedly: "expressed in the words of our language." Originally all rules and teachings of spiritual science were expressed in a symbolical sign-language, some understanding of which must be acquired before its whole meaning and scope can be realized. This understanding is dependent on the first steps toward higher knowledge, and these steps result from the exact observation of such rules as are here given. For all who earnestly will, the path stands, open to tread.

Simple, in truth, is the above rule concerning moments of inner tranquillity; equally simple is its observation. But it only achieves its purpose when it is observed in as earnest and strict a manner as it is, in itself, simple. How this rule is to be observed will, therefore, be explained without digression.

The student must set aside a small part of his daily life in which to concern himself with something quite different from the objects of his daily occupation. The way, also, in which he occupies himself at such a time must differ entirely from the way in which he performs the rest of his daily duties. But this does not mean that what he does in the time thus set apart has no connection with his daily work. On the contrary, he will soon find that just these secluded moments, when sought in the right way, give him full power to perform his daily task. Nor must it be supposed that the observance of this rule will really encroach upon the time needed for the performance of his duties. Should anyone really have

20

no more time at his disposal, five minutes a day will suffice. It all depends on the manner in which these five minutes are spent.

During these periods the student should wrest himself entirely free from his work-a-day life. His thoughts and feelings should take on a different coloring. His joys and sorrows, his cares, experiences and actions must pass in review before his soul; and he must adopt such a position that he may regard all his sundry experiences from a higher point of view.

We need only bear in mind how, in ordinary life, we regard the experiences and actions of others quite differently from our own. This cannot be otherwise, for we are interwoven with our own actions and experiences, whereas those of others we only contemplate. Our aim in these moments of seclusion must be so to contemplate and judge our own actions and experiences as though they applied not to ourselves but to some other person. Suppose, for example, a heavy misfortune befalls us. How different would be our attitude toward a similar misfortune had it befallen our neighbor. This attitude cannot be blamed as unjustifiable; it is part of human nature, and applies equally to exceptional circumstances and to the daily affairs of life. The student must seek the power of confronting himself, at certain times, as a stranger. He must stand before himself with the inner tranquillity of a judge. When this is attained, our own experiences present themselves in a new light. As long as we are interwoven with them and stand, as it were, within them, we cling to the non-essential just as much as to the essential. If we attain the calm inner survey, the essential is severed from the non-essential. Sorrow and joy, every thought, every resolve, appear different when we confront ourselves in this way. It is as though we had spent the whole day in a place where we beheld the smallest objects at the same close range as the largest, and in the evening climbed a neighboring hill and surveyed the whole scene at a glance. Then the various parts appear related to each other in different proportions from those they bore when seen from within. This exercise will not and need not succeed with present occurrences of destiny, but it should be attempted by the student in connection with the events of destiny already experienced in the past. The value of such inner tranquil self-contemplation depends far less on what is actually contemplated than on our finding within ourselves the power which such inner tranquillity develops.

For every human being bears a higher man within himself besides what we may call the work-a-day man. This higher man remains hidden until he is awakened. And each human being can himself alone awaken this higher being within himself. As long as this higher being is not awakened, the higher faculties slumbering in every human being, and leading to supersensible knowledge, will remain concealed. The student must resolve to persevere in the strict and earnest observation of the rule here given, so long as he does not feel within himself the fruits of this inner tranquillity. To all who thus persevere the day will come when spiritual light will envelop them, and a new world will be revealed to an organ of sight of whose presence within them they were never aware.

And no change need take place in the outward life of the student in consequence of this new rule. He performs his duties and, at first, feels the same joys, sorrows, and experiences as before. In no way can it estrange him from life; he can rather devote himself the more thoroughly to this life for the remainder of the day, having gained a higher life in the moments set apart. Little by little this higher life will make its influence felt on his ordinary life. The tranquillity of the moments set apart will also affect everyday existence. In his whole being he will grow calmer; he will attain firm assurance in all his actions, and cease to be put out of countenance by all manner of incidents. By thus advancing he will gradually become more and more his own guide, and allow himself less and less to be led by circumstances and external influences. He will soon discover how great a source of strength is available to him in these moments thus set apart. He will begin no longer to get angry at things which formerly annoyed him; countless things he formerly feared cease to alarm him. He acquires a new outlook on life. Formerly he may have approached some occupation in a faint-hearted way. He would say: "Oh, I lack the power to do this as well as I could wish." Now this thought does not occur to him, but rather a quite different thought. Henceforth he says to himself: "I will summon all my strength to do my work as well as I possibly can." And he suppresses the thought which makes him faint-hearted; for he knows that this very thought might be the cause of a worse performance on his part, and that in any case it cannot contribute to the improvement of his work. And thus thought after thought, each fraught with advantage to his whole life, flows into the student's outlook. They take the place of those that had a hampering, weakening effect. He begins to steer his own ship on a secure course through the waves of life, whereas it was formerly battered to and fro by these waves.

This calm and serenity react on the whole being. They assist the growth of the inner man, and, with the inner man, those faculties also grow which lead to higher knowledge. For it is by his progress in this direction that the student gradually reaches the point where he himself determines the manner in which the impressions of the outer world shall affect him. Thus he may hear a word spoken with the object of wounding or vexing him. Formerly it would indeed have wounded or vexed him, but now that he treads the path to higher knowledge, he is able—before the word has found its way to his inner self—to take from it the sting which gives it the power to wound or vex. Take another example. We easily become impatient when we are kept waiting, but—if we tread the path to higher knowledge—we so steep ourselves in our moments of calm with the feeling of the uselessness of impatience that henceforth, on every occasion of impatience, this feeling is immediately present within us. The impatience that was about to make itself felt vanishes, and an interval which would otherwise have been wasted in expressions of impatience will be filled by useful observation, which can be made while waiting.

Now, the scope and significance of these facts must be realized. We must bear in mind that the higher man within us is in constant development. But only the state of calm and serenity here described renders an orderly development possible. The waves of outward life constrain the inner man from all sides if, instead of mastering this outward life, it masters him. Such a man is like a plant which tries to expand in a cleft in the rock and is stunted in its growth until new

26

space is given it. No outward forces can supply space to the inner man. It can only be supplied by the inner calm which man himself gives to his soul. Outward circumstances can only alter the course of his outward life; they can never awaken the inner spiritual man. The student must himself give birth to a new and higher man within himself.

This higher man now becomes the inner ruler who directs the circumstances of the outer man with sure guidance. As long as the outer man has the upper hand and control, this inner man is his slave and therefore cannot unfold his powers. If it depends on something other than myself whether I should get angry or not, I am not master of myself, or, to put it better, I have not yet found the ruler within myself. I must develop the faculty of letting the impressions of the outer world approach me only in the way in which I myself determine; then only do I become in the real sense a student. And only in as far as the student earnestly seeks this power can he reach the goal. It is of no importance how far anyone can go in a given time; the point is that he should earnestly seek. Many have striven for years without noticing any appreciable progress; but many of those who did not despair, but remained unshaken, have then quite suddenly achieved the inner victory.

No doubt a great effort is required in many stations of life to provide these moments of inner calm; but the greater the effort needed, the more important is the achievement. In spiritual science everything depends upon the energy, inward truthfulness, and uncompromising sincerity with which we confront our own selves, with all our deeds and actions, as a complete stranger.

But only one side of the student's inner activity is characterized by this birth of his own higher being. Something else is needed in addition. Even if he confronts himself as a stranger it is only himself that he contemplates; he looks on those experiences and actions with which he is connected through his particular station of life. He must now disengage himself from it and rise beyond to a purely human level, which no longer has anything to do with his own special situation. He must pass on to the contemplation of those things which would concern him as a human being, even if he lived under quite different circumstances and in quite a different situation. In this way something begins to live within him which ranges above the purely personal. His gaze is directed to worlds higher than those with which every-day life connects him. And thus he begins to feel and realize, as an inner experience, that he belongs to those higher worlds. These are worlds concerning which his senses and his daily occupation can tell him nothing. Thus he now shifts the central point of his being to the inner part of his nature. He listens to the voices within him which speak to him in his moments of tranquillity; he cultivates an intercourse with the spiritual world. He is removed from the every-day world. Its noise is silenced. All around him there is silence. He puts away everything that reminds him of such impressions from without. Calm inward contemplation and converse with the purely spiritual world fill his soul.—Such tranquil contemplation must become a natural necessity in the life of the student. He is now plunged in a world of thought. He must develop a living feeling for this silent thought-activity. He must learn to love what the spirit pours into him. He will soon cease to feel that this thought-world is less real than the every-day things which surround him. He begins to deal with his thoughts as with things in space, and the moment approaches when he begins to feel that which reveals itself in the silent inward thought-work to be much higher, much more real, than the things in space. He discovers that something living expresses itself in this thought-world. He sees that his thoughts do not merely harbor shadow-pictures, but that through them hidden beings speak to him. Out of the silence, speech becomes audible to him. Formerly sound only reached him through his ear; now it resounds through his soul. An inner language, an inner word is revealed to him. This moment, when first experienced, is one of greatest rapture for the student. An inner light is shed over the whole external world, and a second life begins for him. Through his being there pours a divine stream from a world of divine rapture.

This life of the soul in thought, which gradually widens into a life in spiritual being, is called by Gnosis and by Spiritual Science, *Meditation* (contemplative reflection). This meditation is the means to supersensible knowledge. But the

30

student in such moments must not merely indulge in feelings; he must not have indefinite sensations in his soul. That would only hinder him from reaching true spiritual knowledge. His thoughts must be clear, sharp and definite, and he will be helped in this if he does not cling blindly to the thoughts that rise within him. Rather must he permeate himself with the lofty thoughts by which men already advanced and possessed of the spirit were inspired at such moments. He should start with the writings which themselves had their origin in just such revelation during meditation. In the mystic, gnostic, and spiritual scientific literature of today the student will find such writings, and in them the material for his meditation. The seekers of the spirit have themselves set down in such writings the thoughts of the divine science which the Spirit has directed his messengers to proclaim to the world.

Through such meditation a complete transformation takes place in the student. He begins to form quite new conceptions of reality. All things acquire a fresh value for him. It cannot be repeated too often that this transformation does not alienate him from the world. He will in no way be estranged from his daily tasks and duties, for he comes to realize that the most insignificant action he has to accomplish, the most insignificant experience which offers itself to him, stands in connection with cosmic beings and cosmic events. When once this connection is revealed to him in his moments of contemplation, he comes to his daily activities with a new, fuller power. For now he knows that his labor and his suffering are given and endured for the sake of a great, spiritual, cosmic whole. Not weariness, but strength to live springs from meditation.

With firm step the student passes through life. No matter what it may bring him, he goes forward erect. In the past he knew not why he labored and suffered, but now he knows. It is obvious that such meditation leads more surely to the goal if conducted under the direction of experienced persons who know of themselves how everything may best be done; and their advice and guidance should be sought. Truly, no one loses his freedom thereby. What would otherwise be mere uncertain groping in the dark becomes under this direction purposeful work. All who apply to those possessing knowledge and experience in these matters will never apply in vain, only they must realize that what they seek is the advice of a friend, not the domination of a would-be ruler. It will always be found that they who really know are the most modest of men, and that nothing is further from their nature than what is called the lust for power.

When, by means of meditation, a man rises to union with the spirit, he brings to life the eternal in him, which is limited by neither birth nor death. The existence of this eternal being can only be doubted by those who have not themselves experienced it. Thus meditation is the way which also leads man to the knowledge, to the contemplation of his eternal, indestructible, essential being; and it is only through meditation that man can attain to such knowledge. Gnosis and Spiritual Science tell of the eternal nature of this being and of its reincarnation. The question is often asked: Why does a man know nothing of his experiences beyond the borders of life and death? Not thus should we ask, but rather: How can we attain such knowledge? In right meditation the path is opened. This alone can revive the memory of experiences beyond the border of life and death. Everyone can attain this knowledge; in each one of us lies the faculty of recognizing and contemplating for ourselves what genuine Mysticism, Spiritual Science, Anthroposophy, and Gnosis teach. Only the right means must be chosen. Only a being with ears and eyes can apprehend sounds and colors; nor can the eye perceive if the light which makes things visible is wanting. Spiritual Science gives the means of developing the spiritual ears and eyes, and of kindling the spiritual light; and this method of spiritual training may be described as consisting of three stages: (1) *Preparation;* this develops the spiritual senses. (2) *Enlightenment;* this kindles the spiritual light. (3) *Initiaation;* this establishes intercourse with the higher spiritual beings.

II

THE STAGES OF INITIATION

THE information given in the following chapters constitutes steps in an esoteric training, the name and character of which will be understood by all who apply this information in the right way. It refers to the three stages through which the training of the spiritual life leads to a certain degree of initiation. But only so much will here be explained as can be publicly imparted. These are merely indications extracted from a still deeper and more intimate doctrine. In esoteric training itself a quite definite course of instruction is followed. Certain exercises enable the soul to attain to a conscious intercourse with the spiritual world. These exercises bear about the same relation to what will be imparted in the following pages, as the instruction given in a higher, strictly disciplined school bears to the incidental teaching in a preparatory school. And yet the earnest and persevering pursuit of the course here indicated will lead to a genuine esoteric training. But impatient dabbling, devoid of earnest perseverance, can lead to nothing at all. The study of Spiritual Science can only be successful if the student retain what has already been indicated in the preceding chapter, and on the basis of this proceed further.

The three stages which the above-mentioned tradition specifies, are as follows: (1) *preparation;* (2) *enlightenment;* (3) *initiation.* It is not altogether necessary that the first of these three stages should be completed before the second can be begun, nor that the second, in turn, be completed before the third be started. In certain respects it is possible to partake of enlightenment, and even of initiation, and in other respects still be in the preparatory stage. Yet it will be necessary to spend a certain time in the stage of preparation before any enlightenment can begin; and, at least in some respects, enlightenment must be completed before it is even possible to enter upon the stage of initiation. But in describing them it

36

is necessary, for the sake of clarity, that the three stages be made to follow in order.

Preparation

Preparation consists in a strict and definite cultivation of the life of thought and feeling, through which the psycho-spiritual body becomes equipped with higher senses and organs of activity in the same way that natural forces have fitted the physical body with organs built out of indeterminate living matter.

To begin with, the attention of the soul is directed to certain events in the world that surrounds us. Such events are, on the one hand, life that is budding, growing, and flourishing, and on the other hand, all phenomena connected with fading, decaying, and withering. The student can observe these events simultaneously, wherever he turns his eyes, and on every occasion they naturally evoke in him feelings and thoughts; but in ordinary circumstances he does not devote himself sufficiently to them. He hurries on too quickly from impression to impression. It is necessary, therefore, that he should fix his attention intently and consciously upon these phenomena. Wherever he observes a definite kind of blooming and flourishing, he must banish everything else from his soul, and entirely surrender himself, for a short time, to this one impression. He will soon convince himself that a feeling which heretofore, in a similar case, would merely have flitted through his soul, now swells out and assumes a powerful and energetic form. He must now allow this feeling to reverberate quietly within himself, while keeping inwardly quite still. He must cut himself off from the outer world, and simply and solely follow what his soul tells him of this blossoming and flourishing.

Yet it must not be thought that much progress can be made if the senses are blunted to the world. First look at the things as keenly and as intently as you possibly can; then only let the feeling which expands to life, and the thought which arises in the soul, take possession of you. The point is that the attention should be directed with perfect inner balance upon both phenomena. If the necessary tranquillity be attained and you surrender yourself to the feeling which expands to life in the soul, then, in due time, the following experience will ensue. Thoughts and feelings of a new kind and unknown before will be noticed uprising in the soul. Indeed, the more often the attention be fixed alternately upon something growing, blossoming, and flourishing, and upon something else that is fading and decaying, the more vivid will these feelings become. And just as the eyes and ears of the physical body are built by natural forces out of living matter, so will the organs of clairvoyance build themselves out of the feelings and thoughts thus evoked. A quite definite form of feeling is connected with growth and expansion, and another equally definite with all that is fading and decaying. But this is only the case if the effort be made to cultivate these feelings in the way indicated. It is possible to describe approximately what these feelings are like. A full conception of them is within the reach of all who undergo these inner experiences.

If the attention be frequently fixed on the phenomena of growing, blooming and flourishing, a feeling remotely allied to the sensation of a sunrise will ensue, while the phenomena of fading and decaying will produce an experience comparable, in the same way, to the slow rising of the moon on the horizon. Both these feelings are forces which, when duly cultivated and developed to ever increasing intensity, lead to the most significant spiritual results. A new world is opened to the student if he systematically and deliberately surrenders himself to such feelings. The soul-world, the so-called astral plane, begins to dawn upon him. Growth and decay are no longer facts which make indefinite impressions on him as of old, but rather they form themselves into spiritual lines and figures of which he had previously suspected nothing. And these lines and figures have, for the different phenomena, different forms. A blooming flower, an animal in the process of growth, a tree that is decaying, evoke in his soul different lines. The soul world (astral plane) broadens out slowly before him. These lines and figures are in no sense arbitrary. Two students who have reached the corresponding stage of development will always see the same lines and figures under the same conditions. Just as a round table will be seen as round by two normal persons, and not as round by one and square by the other, so too, at the sight of a flower, the same spiritual figure is presented to the soul. And just as the

40

forms of animals and plants are described in ordinary natural history, so too, the spiritual scientist describes or draws the spiritual forms of the process of growth and decay, according to species and kind.

If the student has progressed so far that he can perceive the spiritual forms of those phenomena which are physically visible to his external sight, he is then not far from the stage where he will behold things which have no physical existence, and which therefore remain entirely hidden (occult) from those who have not received suitable instruction and training.

It should be emphasized that the student must never lose himself in speculations on the meaning of one thing or another. Such intellectualizing will only draw him away from the right road. He should look out on the world with keen, healthy senses and quickened power of observation, and then give himself up to the feeling that arises within him. He should not try to make out, through intellectual speculation, the meaning of things, but rather allow the things to disclose themselves. It should be remarked that artistic feeling, when coupled with a quiet introspective nature, forms the best preliminary condition for the development of spiritual faculties. This feeling pierces through the superficial aspect of things, and, in so doing touches their secrets.

A further point of importance is what spiritual science calls *orientation* in the higher worlds. This is attained when the student is permeated, through and through, with the conscious realization that feelings and thoughts are just as much veritable realities as are tables and chairs in the world of the physical senses. In the soul and thought world, feelings and thoughts react upon each other just as do physical objects in the physical world. As long as the student is not vividly permeated with this consciousness, he will not believe that a wrong thought in his mind may have as devastating an effect upon other thoughts that spread life in the thought world as the effect wrought by a bullet fired at random upon the physical objects it hits. He will perhaps never allow himself to perform a physically visible action which he considers to be wrong, though he will not shrink from harboring wrong thoughts and feelings, for these appear harmless to the rest of the world. There can be no progress, however, on

42

the path to higher knowledge unless we guard our thoughts and feelings in just the same way we guard our steps in the physical world. If we see a wall before us, we do not attempt to dash right through it, but turn aside. In other words, we guide ourselves by the laws of the physical world. There are such laws, too, for the soul and thought world, only they cannot impose themselves on us from without. They must flow out of the life of the soul itself. This can be attained if we forbid ourselves to harbor wrong thoughts and feelings. All arbitrary flitting to and fro in thought, all accidental ebbing and flowing of emotion must be forbidden in the same way. In so doing we do not become deficient in feeling. On the contrary, if we regulate our inner life in this way, we shall soon find ourselves becoming rich in feelings and creative with genuine imagination. In the place of petty emotionalism and capricious flights of thought, there appear significant emotions and thoughts that are fruitful. Feelings and thoughts of this kind lead the student to orientation in the spiritual world. He gains a right position in relation to the things of the spiritual world; a distinct and definite result comes into effect in his favor.

43

Just as he, as a physical man, finds his way among physical things, so, too, his path now leads him between growth and decay, which he has already come to know in the way described above. On the one hand, he follows all processes of growing and flourishing and, on the other, of withering and decaying in a way that is necessary for his own and the world's advancement.

The student has also to bestow a further care on the world of sound. He must discriminate between sounds that are produced by the so-called inert (lifeless) bodies, for instance, a bell, or a musical instrument, or a falling mass, and those which proceed from a living creature (an animal or a human being). When a bell is struck, we hear the sound and connect a pleasant feeling with it; but when we hear the cry of an animal, we can, besides our own feeling, detect through it the manifestation of an inward experience of the animal, whether of pleasure or of pain. It is with the latter kind of sound that the student sets to work. He must concentrate his whole attention on the fact that the sound tells him of something that lies outside his own soul. He must immerse himself in this foreign thing. He must closely

44

unite his own feeling with the pleasure or pain of which the sound tells him. He must get beyond the point of caring whether, for him, the sound is pleasant or unpleasant, agreeable or disagreeable, and his soul must be filled with whatever is occurring in the being from which the sound proceeds. Through such exercises, if systematically and deliberately performed, the student will develop within himself the faculty of intermingling, as it were, with the being from which the sound proceeds. A person sensitive to music will find it easier than one who is unmusical to cultivate his inner life in this way; but no one should suppose that a mere sense for music can take the place of this inner activity. The student must learn to feel in this way in the face of the whole of nature. This implants a new faculty in his world of thought and feeling. Through her resounding tones, the whole of nature begins to whisper her secrets to the student. What was hitherto merely incomprehensible noise to his soul becomes by this means a coherent language of nature. And whereas hitherto he only heard sound from the so-called inanimate objects, he now is aware of a new language of the soul. Should he advance further

45

in this inner culture, he will soon learn that he can hear what hitherto he did not even surmise. He begins to hear with the soul.

To this, one thing more must be added before the highest point in this region can be attained. Of very great importance for the development of the student is the way in which he listens to others when they speak. He must accustom himself to do this in such a way that, while listening, his inner self is absolutely silent. If someone expresses an opinion and another listens, assent or dissent will, generally speaking, stir in the inner self of the listener. Many people in such cases feel themselves impelled to an expression of their assent, or, more especially, of their dissent. In the student, all such assent or dissent must be silenced. It is not imperative that he should suddenly alter his way of living by trying to attain at all times to this complete inner silence. He will have to begin by doing so in special cases, deliberately selected by himself. Then quite slowly and by degrees, this new way of listening will creep into his habits, as of itself. In spiritual research this is systematically practiced. The student feels it his duty to listen, by way of practice, at certain

46

times to the most contradictory views and, at the same time, bring entirely to silence all assent, and more especially, all adverse criticism. The point is that in so doing, not only all purely intellectual judgment be silenced, but also all feelings of displeasure, denial, or even assent. The student must at all times be particularly watchful lest such feelings, even when not on the surface, should still lurk in the innermost recess of the soul. He must listen, for example, to the statements of people who are, in some respects, far beneath him, and yet while doing so suppress every feeling of greater knowledge or superiority. It is useful for everyone to listen in this way to children, for even the wisest can learn incalculably much from children. The student can thus train himself to listen to the words of others quite selflessly, completely shutting out his own person and his opinions and way of feeling. When he practices listening without criticism, even when a completely contradictory opinion is advanced, when the most hopeless mistake is committed before him, he then learns, little by little, to blend himself with the being of another and become identified with it. Then he hears through the words into

47

the soul of the other. Through continued exercise of this kind, sound becomes the right medium for the perception of soul and spirit. Of course it implies the very strictest self-discipline, but the latter leads to a high goal. When these exercises are practiced in connection with the other already given, dealing with the sounds of nature, the soul develops a new sense of hearing. She is now able to perceive manifestations from the spiritual world which do not find their expression in sounds perceptible to the physical ear. The perception of the "inner word" awakens. Gradually truths reveal themselves to the student from the spiritual world. He hears speech uttered to him in a spiritual way. Only to those who, by selfless listening, train themselves to be really receptive from within, in stillness, unmoved by personal opinion or feeling, only to such can the higher beings speak of whom spiritual science tells. As long as one hurls any personal opinion or feeling against the speaker to whom one must listen, the beings of the spiritual world remain silent.

All higher truths are attained through such inwardly instilled speech, and what we hear from the lips of a true spiritual teacher has been experienced by him in this manner. But this does not mean that it is unimportant for us to acquaint ourselves with the writings of spiritual science before we can ourselves hear such inwardly instilled speech. On the contrary, the reading of such writings and the listening to the teachings of spiritual science are themselves means of attaining personal knowledge. Every sentence of spiritual science we hear is of a nature to direct the mind to the point which must be reached before the soul can experience real progress. To the practice of all that has here been indicated must be added the ardent study of what the spiritual researchers impart to the world. In all esoteric training such study belongs to the preparatory period, and all other methods will prove ineffective if due receptivity for the teachings of the spiritual researcher is lacking. For since these instructions are culled from the living inner word, from the living inwardly instilled speech, they are themselves gifted with spiritual life. They are not mere words; they are living powers. And while you follow the words of one who knows, while you read a book that springs from real inner experience, powers are at work in your soul which make you clairvoyant, just as natural forces have created out of living matter your eyes and your ears.

Enlightenment

Enlightenment proceeds from very simple processes. Here, too, it is a matter of developing certain feelings and thoughts which slumber in every human being and must be awakened. It is only when these simple processes are carried out with unfailing patience, continuously and conscientiously, that they can lead to the perception of the inner light-forms. The first step is taken by observing different natural objects in a particular way; for instance, a transparent and beautifully formed stone (a crystal), a plant, and an animal. The student should endeavor, at first, to direct his whole attention to a comparison of the stone with the animal in the following manner. The thoughts here mentioned should pass through his soul accompanied by vivid feelings, and no other thought, no other feeling, must mingle with them and disturb what should be an intensely

50

attentive observation. The student says to himself: "The stone has a form; the animal also has a form. The stone remains motionless in its place. The animal changes its place. It is instinct (desire) which causes the animal to change its place. Instincts, too, are served by the form of the animal. Its organs and limbs are fashioned in accordance with these instincts. The form of the stone is not fashioned in accordance with desires, but in accordance with desireless force." (The fact here mentioned, in its bearing on the contemplation of crystals, is in many ways distorted by those who have only heard of it in an outward, exoteric manner, and in this way such practices as crystal-gazing have their origin. Such manipulations are based on a misunderstanding. They have been described in many books, but they never form the subject of genuine esoteric teaching.)

By sinking deeply into such thoughts, and while doing so, observing the stone and the animal with rapt attention, there arise in the soul two quite separate kinds of feelings. From the stone there flows into the soul the one kind of feeling, and from the animal the other kind. The attempt will probably not succeed at first, but little by little, with genuine and patient practice, these feelings ensue. Only, this exercise must be practiced over and over again. At first the feelings are only present as long as the observation lasts. Later on they continue, and then they grow to something which remains living in the soul. The student has then but to reflect, and both feelings will always arise, even without the contemplation of an external object. Out of these feelings and the thoughts that are bound up with them, the organs of clairvoyance are formed. If the plant should then be included in this observation, it will be noticed that the feeling flowing from it lies between the feelings derived from the stone and the animal, in both quality and degree. The organs thus formed are spiritual eyes. The student gradually learns, by their means, to see something like soul and spirit colors. The spiritual world with its lines and figures remains dark as long as he has only attained what has been described as preparation; through enlightenment this world becomes light. Here it must also be noted that the words "dark" and "light," as well as the other expressions used, only approximately describe what is meant. This cannot be otherwise if ordinary language is used, for this language was created to suit physical conditions. Spiritual science describes that which, for clairvoyant organs, flows from the stone, as blue, or blue-red; and that which is felt as coming from the animal as red or red-yellow. In reality, colors of a spiritual kind are seen. The color proceeding from the plant is green which little by little turns into a light ethereal pink. The plant is actually that product of nature which in higher worlds resembles, in certain respects, its constitution in the physical world. The same does not apply to the stone and the animal. It must now be clearly understood that the above-mentioned colors only represent the principal shades in the stone, plant, and animal kingdom. In reality, all possible intermediate shades are present. Every stone, every plant, every animal has its own particular shade of color. In addition to these there are also the beings of the higher worlds who never incarnate physically, but who have their colors, often wonderful, often horrible. Indeed, the wealth of color in these higher worlds is immeasurably greater than in the physical world.

Once the faculty of seeing with spiritual eyes has been acquired, one then encounters sooner or later the beings here mentioned, some of them higher, some lower than man himself—beings that never enter physical reality.

If this point has been reached, the way to a great deal lies open. But it is inadvisable to proceed further without paying careful heed to what is said or otherwise imparted by the spiritual researcher. And for that, too, which has been described, attention paid to such experienced guidance is the very best thing. Moreover, if a man has the strength and the endurance to travel so far that he fulfills the elementary conditions of enlightenment, he will assuredly seek and find the right guidance.

But in any circumstances, one precaution is necessary, failing which it were better to leave untrodden all steps on the path to higher knowledge. It is necessary that the student should lose none of his qualities as a good and noble man, or his receptivity for all physical reality. Indeed, throughout his training he must continually increase his moral strength, his inner purity, and his power of observation. To give an example:

during the elementary exercises on enlightenment, the student must take care always to enlarge his sympathy for the animal and the human worlds, and his sense for the beauty of nature. Failing this care, such exercises would continually blunt that feeling and that sense; the heart would become hardened, and the senses blunted, and that could only lead to perilous results.

How enlightenment proceeds if the student rises, in the sense of the foregoing exercises, from the stone, the plant, and the animal, up to man, and how, after enlightenment, under all circumstances the union of the soul with the spiritual world is effected, leading to initiation—with these things the following chapters will deal, in as far as they can and may do so.

In our time the path to spiritual science is sought by many. It is sought in many ways, and many dangerous and even despicable practices are attempted. It is for this reason that they who claim to know something of the truth in these matters place before others the possibility of learning something of esoteric training. Only so much is here imparted as accords with this possibility. It is necessary that something of the truth

55

should become known, in order to prevent error causing great harm. No harm can come to anyone following the way here described, so long as he does not force matters. Only, one thing should be noted: no student should spend more time and strength upon these exercises than he can spare with due regard to his station in life and to his duties; nor should he change anything, for the time being, in the external conditions of his life through taking this path. Without patience no genuine results can be attained. After doing an exercise for a few minutes, the student must be able to stop and continue quietly his daily work, and no thought of these exercises should mingle with the day's work. No one is of use as an esoteric student or will ever attain results of real value who has not learned to wait in the highest and best sense of the word.

The Control of Thoughts and Feelings

When the student seeks the path leading to higher knowledge in the way described in the preceding chapter, he should not omit to fortify himself, throughout his work, with one ever present thought. He must never cease repeating to himself that he may have made quite considerable progress after a certain interval of time, though it may not be apparent to him in the way he perhaps expected; otherwise he can easily lose heart and abandon all attempts after a short time. The powers and faculties to be developed are of a most subtle kind, and differ entirely in their nature from the conceptions previously formed by the student. He had been accustomed to occupy himself exclusively with the physical world; the world of spirit and soul had been concealed from his vision and concepts. It is therefore not surprising if he does not immediately notice the powers of soul and spirit now developing in him. In this respect there is a possibility of discouragement for those setting out on the path to higher knowledge, if they ignore the experience gathered by responsible investigators. The teacher is aware of the progress made by his pupil long before the latter is conscious of it. He knows how the delicate spiritual eyes begin to form themselves long before the pupil is aware of this, and a great part of what he has to say is couched in such terms as to prevent the pupil from losing patience and perseverance before he can himself gain knowledge of his own progress. The teacher, as we know, can confer upon the pupil no powers which are not already latent within him, and his sole function is to assist in the awakening of slumbering faculties. But what he imparts out of his own experience is a pillar of strength for the one wishing to penetrate through darkness to light. Many abandon the path to higher knowledge soon after having set foot upon it, because their progress is not immediately apparent to them. And even when the first experiences begin to dawn upon the pupil, he is apt to regard them as illusions, because he had formed quite different conceptions of what he was going to experience. He loses courage, either because he regards these first experiences as being of no value, or because they appear to him to be so insignificant that he cannot believe they will lead him to any appreciable results within a measurable time. Courage and self-confidence are two beacons which must never be extinguished on the path to higher knowledge. No one will ever travel far who cannot bring himself to repeat, over and over again, an exercise which has failed, apparently, for a countless number of times.

Long before any distinct perception of progress, there rises in the student, from the hidden depths of the soul, a feeling that he is on the right path. This feeling should be cherished and fostered, for it can develop into a trustworthy guide. Above all, it is imperative to extirpate the idea that any fantastic, mysterious practices are required for the attainment of higher knowledge. It must be clearly realized that a start has to be made with the thoughts and feelings with which we continually live, and that these feelings and thoughts must merely be given a new direction. Everyone must say to himself: *"In my own world of thought and feeling the deepest mysteries lie hidden, only hitherto I have been unable to perceive them."* In the end it all resolves itself into the fact that man ordinarily carries body, soul, and spirit about with him, and yet is conscious in a true sense only of his body, and not of his soul and spirit. The student becomes conscious of soul and spirit, just as the ordinary person is conscious of his body. Hence it is highly important to give the

59

proper direction to thoughts and feelings, for then only can the perception be developed of all that is invisible in ordinary life. One of the ways by which this development may be carried out will now be indicated. Again, like almost everything else so far explained, it is quite a simple matter. Yet its results are of the greatest consequence, if the necessary devotion and sympathy be applied.

Let the student place before himself the small seed of a plant, and while contemplating this insignificant object, form with intensity the right kind of thoughts, and through these thoughts develop certain feelings. In the first place let him clearly grasp what he really sees with his eyes. Let him describe to himself the shape, color, and all other qualities of the seed. Then let his mind dwell upon the following train of thought: *"Out of the seed, if planted in the soil, a plant of complex structure will grow."* Let him build up this plant in his imagination, and reflect as follows: *"What I am now picturing to myself in my imagination will later on be enticed from the seed by the forces of earth and light. If I had before me an artificial object which imitated the seed to*

60

such a deceptive degree that my eyes could not distinguish it from a real seed, no forces of earth or light could avail to produce from it a plant." If the student thoroughly grasps this thought so that it becomes an inward experience, he will also be able to form the following thought and couple it with the right feeling: *"All that will ultimately grow out of the seed is now secretly enfolded within it as the force of the whole plant. In the artificial imitation of the seed there is no such force present. And yet both appear alike to my eyes. The real seed, therefore, contains something invisible which is not present in the imitation."* It is on this invisible something that thought and feeling are to be concentrated. (Anyone objecting that a microscopical examination would reveal the difference between the real seed and the imitation would only show that he had failed to grasp the point. The intention is not to investigate the physical nature of the object, but to use it for the development of psycho-spiritual forces.)

Let the student fully realize that this invisible something will transmute itself later on into a visible plant, which he will have before him in its

shape and color. Let him ponder on the thought:
*"The invisible will become visible. If I could not
think, then that which will only become visible
later on could not already make its presence felt
to me."* Particular stress must be laid on the following point: what the student thinks he must
also feel with intensity. In inner tranquillity, the
thought mentioned above must become a conscious inner experience, to the exclusion of all
other thoughts and disturbances. And sufficient
time must be taken to allow the thought and the
feeling which is coupled with it to bore themselves into the soul, as it were. If this be accomplished in the right way, then, after a time—possibly not until after numerous attempts—an inner
force will make itself felt. This force will create
new powers of perception. The grain of seed will
appear as if enveloped in a small luminous cloud.
In a sensible-supersensible way, it will be felt as
a kind of flame. The center of this flame evokes
the same feeling that one has when under the impression of the color lilac, and the edges as when
under the impression of a bluish tone. What was
formerly invisible now becomes visible, for it is
created by the power of the thoughts and the feel-

62

ings we have stirred to life within ourselves. The plant itself will not become visible until later, so that the physically invisible now reveals itself in a spiritually visible way.

It is not surprising that all this appears to many as illusion. "What is the use of such visions," they ask, "and such hallucinations?" And many will thus fall away and abandon the path. But this is precisely the important point: not to confuse spiritual reality with imagination at this difficult stage of human evolution, and furthermore, to have the courage to press onward and not become timorous and faint-hearted. On the other hand, however, the necessity must be emphasized of maintaining unimpaired and of perpetually cultivating that healthy sound sense which distinguishes truth from illusion. Fully conscious self-control must never be lost during all these exercises, and they must be accompanied by the same sane, sound thinking which is applied to the details of every-day life. To lapse into reveries would be fatal. The intellectual clarity, not to say the sobriety of thought, must never for a moment be dulled. The greatest mistake would be made if the student's mental balance were disturbed through such exercises, if he were hampered in judging the matters of his daily life as sanely and as soundly as before. He should examine himself again and again to find out if he has remained unaltered in relation to the circumstances among which he lives, or whether he may perhaps have become unbalanced. Above all, strict care must be taken not to drift at random into vague reveries, or to experiment with all kinds of exercises. The trains of thought here indicated have been tested and practiced in esoteric training since the earliest times, and only such are given in these pages. Anyone attempting to use others devised by himself, or of which he may have heard or read at one place or another, will inevitably go astray and find himself on the path of boundless chimera.

As a further exercise to succeed the one just described, the following may be taken: Let the student place before him a plant which has attained the stage of full development. Now let him fill his mind with the thought that the time will come when this plant will wither and die. *"Nothing will be left of what I now see before me. But this plant will have developed seeds which, in their turn, will develop to new plants. I again become aware that in what I see, something lies hidden which I cannot see. I fill my mind entirely with the thought: this plant, with its form and colors, will in time be no more. But the reflection that it produces seeds teaches me that it will not disappear into nothing. I cannot at present see with my eyes that which guards it from disappearance, any more than I previously could discern the plant in the grain of seed. Thus there is something in the plant which my eyes cannot see. If I let this thought live within me, and if the corresponding feeling be coupled with it, then, in due time, there will again develop in my soul a force which will ripen into a new perception."* Out of the plant there again grows a kind of spiritual flame-form, which is, of course, correspondingly larger than the one previously described. The flame can be felt as being greenish-blue in the center, and yellowish-red at the outer edge.

It must be explicitly emphasized that the colors here described are not seen as the physical eyes see colors, but that through spiritual perception the same feeling is experienced as in the case of a physical color-impression. To apprehend blue

65

spiritually means to have a sensation similar to the one experienced when the physical eye rests on the color blue. This fact must be noted by all who intend to rise to spiritual perception. Otherwise they will expect a mere repetition of the physical in the spiritual. This could only lead to the bitterest deception.

Anyone having reached this point of spiritual vision is the richer by a great deal, for he can perceive things not only in their present state of being but also in their process of growth and decay. He begins to see in all things the spirit, of which physical eyes can know nothing. And therewith he has taken the first step toward the gradual solution, through personal vision, of the secret of birth and death. For the outer senses a being comes into existence through birth, and passes away through death. This, however, is only because these senses cannot perceive the concealed spirit of the being. For the spirit, birth and death are merely a transformation, just as the unfolding of the flower from the bud is a transformation enacted before our physical eyes. But if we desire to learn this through personal vision we must

66

first awaken the requisite spiritual sense in the way here indicated.

In order to meet another objection, which may be raised by certain people who have some psychic experience, let it at once be admitted that there are shorter and simpler ways, and that there are persons who have acquired knowledge of the phenomena of birth and death through personal vision, without first going through all that has here been described. There are, in fact, people with considerable psychic gifts who need but a slight impulse in order to find themselves already developed. But they are the exceptions, and the methods described above are safer and apply equally to all. It is possible to acquire some knowledge of chemistry in an exceptional way, but if you wish to become a chemist you must follow the recognized and reliable course.

An error fraught with serious consequences would ensue if it were assumed that the desired result could be reached more easily if the grain of seed or the plant mentioned above were merely imagined, were merely pictured in the imagination. This might lead to results, but not so surely as the method here given. The vision thus attained would, in most cases, be a mere figment of the imagination, the transformation of which into genuine spiritual vision would still remain to be accomplished. It is not intended arbitrarily to create visions, but to allow reality to create them within oneself. The truth must well up from the depths of our own soul; it must not be conjured forth by our ordinary ego, but by the beings themselves whose spiritual truth we are to contemplate.

Once the student has found the beginnings of spiritual vision by means of such exercises, he may proceed to the contemplation of man himself. Simple phenomena of human life must first be chosen. But before making any attempt in this direction it is imperative for the student to strive for the absolute purity of his moral character. He must banish all thought of ever using knowledge gained in this way for his own personal benefit. He must be convinced that he would never, under any circumstances, avail himself in an evil sense of any power he may gain over his fellow-creatures. For this reason, all who seek to discover through personal vision the secrets in human nature must follow the golden rule of true spiritual science. This golden rule is as follows: *For every one step that you take in the pursuit of higher knowledge, take three steps in the perfection of your own character.* If this rule is observed, such exercises as the following may be attempted:

Recall to mind some person whom you may have observed when he was filled with desire for some object. Direct your attention to this desire. It is best to recall to memory that moment when the desire was at its height, and it was still uncertain whether the object of the desire would be attained. And now fill your mind with this recollection, and reflect on what you can thus observe. Maintain the utmost inner tranquillity. Make the greatest possible effort to be blind and deaf to everything that may be going on around you, and take special heed that through the conception thus evoked a feeling should awaken in your soul. Allow this feeling to rise in your soul like a cloud on the cloudless horizon. As a rule, of course, your reflection will be interrupted, because the person whom it concerns was not observed in this particular state of soul for a sufficient length of time. The attempt will most likely fail hundreds and hundreds of times. It is just a question of not losing patience. After many attempts you will succeed in experiencing a feeling in your soul corresponding to the state of soul of the person observed, and you will begin to notice that through this feeling a power grows in your soul that leads to spiritual insight into the state of soul of the other. A picture experienced as luminous appears in your field of vision. This spiritually luminous picture is the so-called astral embodiment of the desire observed in that soul. Again the impression of this picture may be described as flame-like, yellowish-red in the center, and reddish-blue or lilac at the edges. Much depends on treating such spiritual experiences with great delicacy. The best thing is not to speak to anyone about them except to your teacher, if you have one. Attempted descriptions of such experiences in inappropriate words usually only lead to gross self-deception. Ordinary terms are employed which are not intended for such things, and are therefore too gross and clumsy. The consequence is that in the attempt to clothe the experience in words we are misled into blending the actual experience with all kinds of fantastic delusions. Here again is another important rule for the student: *know how to observe silence concerning your spiritual experiences.* Yes, observe silence even toward yourself. Do not attempt to clothe in words what you contemplate in the spirit, or to pore over it with clumsy intellect. Lend yourself freely and without reservation to these spiritual impressions, and do not disturb them by reflecting and pondering over them too much. For you must remember that your reasoning faculties are, to begin with, by no means equal to your new experience. You have acquired these reasoning faculties in a life hitherto confined to the physical world of the senses; the faculties you are now acquiring transcend this world. Do not try, therefore, to apply to the new and higher perceptions the standard of the old. Only he who has gained some certainty and steadiness in the observation of inner experiences can speak about them, and thereby stimulate his fellow-men.

The exercise just described may be supplemented by the following. *Direct your attention in the same way upon a person to whom the fulfillment of some wish, the gratification of some*

71

desire, has been granted. If the same rules and precautions be adopted as in the previous instance, spiritual insight will once more be attained. A spiritual flame-form will be distinguished, creating an impression of yellow in the center and green at the edges.

By such observation of his fellow-creatures the student may easily lapse into a moral fault. He may become cold-hearted. Every conceivable effort must be made to prevent this. Such observation should only be practiced by one who has already risen to the level on which complete certainty is found that thoughts are real things. He will then no longer allow himself to think of his fellow-men in a way that is incompatible with the highest reverence for human dignity and human liberty. The thought that a human being could be merely an object of observation must never for a moment be entertained. Self-education must see to it that this insight into human nature should go hand in hand with an unlimited respect for the personal privilege of each individual, and with the recognition of the sacred and inviolable nature of that which dwells in each human being. A feeling of reverential awe must fill us, even in our recollections.

For the present, only these two examples can be given to show how enlightened insight into human nature may be achieved; they will at least serve to point out the way to be taken. By gaining the inner tranquillity and repose indispensable for such observation, the student will have undergone a great inner transformation. He will then soon reach the point where this enrichment of his inner self will lend confidence and composure to his outward demeanor. And this transformation of his outward demeanor will again react favorably on his soul. Thus he will be able to help himself further along the road. He will find ways and means of penetrating more and more into the secrets of human nature which are hidden from our external senses, and he will then also become ripe for a deeper insight into the mysterious connections between human nature and all else that exists in the universe. By following this path the student approaches closer and closer to the moment when he can effectively take the first steps of initiation. But before these can be taken, one thing more is necessary, though at first its need will be least of all apparent; later on, however, the student will be convinced of it.

The would-be initiate must bring with him a certain measure of courage and fearlessness. He must positively go out of his way to find opportunities for developing these virtues. His training should provide for their systematic cultivation. In this respect, life itself is a good school—possibly the best school. The student must learn to look danger calmly in the face and try to overcome difficulties unswervingly. For instance, when in the presence of some peril, he must swiftly come to the conviction that fear is of no possible use; I must not feel afraid; I must only think of what is to be done. And he must improve to the extent of feeling, upon occasions which formerly inspired him with fear, that to be frightened, to be disheartened, are things that are out of the question as far as his own inmost self is concerned. By self-discipline in this direction, quite definite qualities are developed which are necessary for initiation into the higher mysteries. Just as man requires nervous force in his physical being in order to use his physical senses, so also he

74

requires in his soul nature the force which is only developed in the courageous and the fearless. For in penetrating to the higher mysteries he will see things which are concealed from ordinary humanity by the illusion of the senses. If the physical senses do not allow us to perceive the higher truth, they are for this very reason our benefactors. Things are thereby hidden from us which, if realized without due preparation, would throw us into unutterable consternation, and the sight of which would be unendurable. The student must be fit to endure this sight. He loses certain supports in the outer world which he owes to the very illusion surrounding him. It is truly and literally as if the attention of someone were called to a danger which had threatened him for a long time, but of which he knew nothing. Hitherto he felt no fear, but now that he knows, he is overcome by fear, though the danger has not been rendered greater by his knowing it.

The forces at work in the world are both destructive and constructive; the destiny of manifested beings is birth and death. The seer is to behold the working of these forces and the march of destiny. The veil enshrouding the spiritual eyes in ordinary life is to be removed. But man is inter-woven with these forces and with this destiny. His own nature harbors destructive and constructive forces. His own soul reveals itself to the seer as un-disguised as the other objects. He must not lose strength in the face of this self-knowledge; but strength will fail him unless he brings a surplus on which to draw. For this purpose he must learn to maintain inner calm and steadiness in the face of difficult circumstances; he must cultivate a strong trust in the beneficent powers of existence. He must be prepared to find that many motives which had actuated him hitherto will do so no longer. He will have to recognize that previously he thought and acted in a certain way only because he was still in the throes of ignorance. Reasons that influenced him formerly will now disappear. He often acted out of vanity; he will now see how utterly futile all vanity is for the seer. He often acted out of greed; he will now become aware how destructive all greed is. He will have to develop quite new motives for his thoughts and actions, and it is just for this purpose that courage and fearlessness are required.

It is pre-eminently a question of cultivating this courage and this fearlessness in the inmost depths of thought-life. The student must learn never to despair over failure. He must be equal to the thought: I shall forget that I have failed in this matter, and I shall try once more as though this had not happened. Thus he will struggle through to the firm conviction that the fountain-head of strength from which he may draw is inexhaustible. He struggles ever onward to the spirit which will uplift him and support him, however weak and impotent his earthly self may have proved. He must be capable of pressing on to the future undismayed by any experiences of the past. If the student has acquired these faculties up to a certain point, he is then ripe to hear the real names of things, which are the key to higher knowledge. For initiation consists in this very act of learning to call the things of the world by those names which they bear in the spirit of their divine authors. In these, their names, lies the mystery of things. It is for this reason that the initiates speak a different language from the uninitiated, for the former know the names by which the beings themselves are called into existence.

In as far as initiation itself can be discussed, this will be done in the following chapter.

III

INITIATION

Initiation is the highest stage in an esoteric training concerning which it is possible to give some indications in a book intended for the general public. Whatever lies beyond forms a subject difficult to understand, yet the way to it can be found by all who have passed through *preparation, enlightenment,* and *initiation* as far as the lesser mysteries.

The knowledge and proficiency conferred by initiation cannot be obtained in any other manner, except in some far distant future, after many incarnations, by quite different means and in quite a different form. The initiate of today undergoes experiences which would otherwise come to him much later, under quite different circumstances.

The secrets of existence are only accessible to an extent corresponding to man's own degree of maturity. For this reason alone the path to the

78

higher stages of knowledge and power is beset
with obstacles. A firearm should not be used until
sufficient experience has been gained to avoid
disaster, caused by its use. A person initiated today
without further ado would lack the experience
which he will gain during his future incarnations
before he can attain to higher knowledge in the
normal course of his development. At the portal
of initiation, therefore, this experience must be
supplied in some other way. Thus the first instructions given to the candidate for initiation
serve as a substitute for these future experiences.
These are the so-called *trials,* which he has to
undergo, and which constitute a normal course of
inner development resulting from due application
to such exercises as are described in the preceding chapters.

These trials are often discussed in books, but
it is only natural that such discussions should as
a rule give quite false impressions of their nature;
for without passing through preparation and enlightenment no one can know anything of these
tests and appropriately describe them.

The would-be initiate must come into contact
with certain things and facts belonging to the

higher worlds, but he can only see and hear them if his feeling is ripe for the perception of the spiritual forms, colors, and tones, described in the chapters on *Preparation* and *Enlightenment*.

The first trial consists in obtaining a truer vision than the average man has of the corporeal attributes of lifeless things, and later of plants, animals, and human beings. This does not mean what at present is called scientific knowledge, for it is a question not of science but of vision. As a rule the would-be initiate proceeds to learn how the objects of nature and the beings gifted with life manifest themselves to the spiritual ear and the spiritual eye. In a certain way these things then lie stripped—naked—before the beholder. The qualities which can then be seen and heard are hidden from the physical eyes and ears. For physical perception they are concealed as if by a veil, and the falling away of this veil for the would-be initiate consists in a process designated as the process of *Purification by Fire*. The first trial is therefore known as the *Fire-Trial*.

For many people, ordinary life is itself a more or less unconscious process of initiation through the *Fire-Trial*. Such people have passed through a wealth of experience, so that their self-confidence, courage and fortitude have been greatly strengthened in a normal manner while learning to bear sorrow, disappointment and failure in their undertakings with greatness of soul, and especially with equanimity and unbroken strength. Thus they are often initiates without knowing it, and it then needs but little to unseal their spiritual hearing and sight so that they become clairvoyant. For it must be noted that a genuine fire-trial is not intended to satisfy the curiosity of the candidate. It is true that he learns many uncommon things of which others can have no inkling, but this acquisition of knowledge is not the end, but the means to the end; the end consists in the attainment, thanks to this knowledge of the higher worlds, of greater and truer self-confidence, a higher degree of courage, and a magnanimity and perseverance such as cannot, as a rule, be acquired in the lower world.

The candidate may always turn back after the fire-trial. He will then resume his life, strengthened in body and soul, and wait for a future incarnation to continue his initiation. In his present incarnation he will prove himself a more useful member of society and of humanity than he was before. In whatever position he may find himself, his firmness, prudence, resoluteness, and his beneficent influence over his fellows will have greatly increased.

But if, after completing the fire-trial, he should wish to continue the path, a certain writing-system generally adopted in esoteric training must now be revealed to him. The actual teachings manifest themselves in this writing, because the hidden (occult) qualities of things cannot be directly expressed in the words of ordinary language; nor can they be set forth in ordinary writing. The pupils of the initiates translate the teachings into ordinary language as best they can. The occult script reveals itself to the soul when the latter has attained spiritual perception, for it is traced in the spiritual world and remains there for all time. It cannot be learned as an artificial writing is learned and read. The candidate grows into clairvoyant knowledge in an appropriate way, and during this growth a new strength is developed in his soul, as a new faculty, through which he feels himself impelled to decipher the occurrences and the beings of the spiritual world

82

like the characters of a writing. This strength, with the experience it brings of the corresponding trial, might possibly awaken in the soul as though of its own accord, as the soul continually develops, but it will be found safer to follow the instructions of those who are spiritually experienced, and who have some proficiency in deciphering the occult script.

The signs of the occult script are not arbitrarily invented; they correspond to the forces actively engaged in the world. They teach us the language of things. It becomes immediately apparent to the candidate that the signs he is now learning correspond to the forms, colors, and tones which he learned to perceive during his preparation and enlightenment. He realizes that all he learned previously was only like learning to spell, and that he is only now beginning to read in the higher worlds. All the isolated figures, tones, and colors reveal themselves to him now in one great connected whole. Now for the first time he attains complete certainty in observing the higher worlds. Hitherto he could never know positively whether the things he saw were rightly seen. A regular understanding, too, is now at last possible between the candidate and the initiate in the spheres of higher knowledge. For whatever form the intercourse between an initiate and another person may take in ordinary life, the higher knowledge in its immediate form can only be imparted by the initiate in the above-mentioned sign-language.

Thanks to this language the student also learns certain rules of conduct and certain duties of which he formerly knew nothing. Having learned these he is able to perform actions endowed with a significance and a meaning such as the actions of one not initiated can never possess. He acts out of the higher worlds. Instructions concerning such action can only be read and understood in the writing in question.

Yet it must be emphasized that there are people unconsciously gifted with the ability and faculty of performing such actions, though they have never undergone an esoteric training. Such helpers of the world and of humanity pass through life bestowing blessings and performing good deeds. For reasons here not to be discussed, gifts have been bestowed on them which appear supernatural. What distinguishes them from the

84

candidate for initiation is only that the latter acts consciously and with full insight into the entire situation. He acquires by training the gifts bestowed on others by higher powers for the good of humanity. We can sincerely revere these favored of God; but we should not for this reason regard the work of esoteric training as superfluous.

Once the student has learned the sign-language there awaits him yet another trial, to prove whether he can move with freedom and assurance in the higher worlds. In ordinary life he is impelled to action by exterior motives. He works at one occupation or another because one duty or another is imposed on him by outward circumstances. It need hardly be mentioned that the student must in no way neglect any of his duties in ordinary life because he is living and working in higher worlds. There is no duty in a higher world that can force a person to neglect any single one of his duties in the ordinary world. The father will remain just as good a father to his family, the mother just as good a mother, and neither the official nor the soldier, nor anyone else will be diverted from his work by becoming an esoteric student. On the contrary, all the qualities which make a human being capable and efficient are enhanced in the student to a degree incomprehensible to the uninitiated. If, in the eyes of the uninitiated, this does not always appear to be the case, it is simply because he often lacks the ability to judge the initiate correctly. The deeds of the latter are not always intelligible to the former. But this only happens in special cases.

At this stage of initiation there are duties to be performed for which no outward stimulus is given. The candidate will not be moved to action by external pressure, but only through adherence to the rules of conduct revealed to him in the occult script. He must now show in this second trial that, led by such rules, he can act with the same firmness and precision with which, for instance, an official performs the duties that belong to him. For this purpose, and in the course of his further training, he will find himself faced by a certain definite task. He must perform some action in consequence of observations made on the basis of what he has learned during preparation and enlightenment. The nature of this action can be understood by means of the occult script with

86

which he is now familiar. If he recognizes his duty and acts rightly, his trial has been successful. The success can be recognized in the alteration produced by his action in the figures, colors, and tones apprehended by his spiritual eyes and ears. Exact indications are given, as the training progresses, showing how these figures appear and are experienced after the action has been performed, and the candidate must know how to produce this change. This trial is known as the *Water-Trial*, because in his activity in these higher worlds the candidate is deprived of the support derived from outward circumstances, as a swimmer is without support when swimming in water that is beyond his depth. This activity must be repeated until the candidate attains absolute poise and assurance.

The importance of this trial lies again in the acquisition of a quality. Through his experiences in the higher worlds, the candidate develops this quality in a short time to such a high degree that he would otherwise have to go through many incarnations, in the ordinary course of his development, before he could acquire it to the same extent. It all centers around the fact that he must be guided only by the results of his higher perception and reading of the occult script, in order to produce the changes in question in these higher regions of existence. Should he, in the course of his activity, introduce any of his own opinions and desires, or should he diverge for one moment from the laws which he has recognized to be right, in order to follow his own wilful inclination, then the result produced would differ entirely from what was intended. He would lose sight of the goal to which his action tended, and confusion would result. Hence ample opportunity is given him in the course of this trial to develop self-control. This is the object in view. Here again, this trial can be more easily passed by those whose life, before initiation, has led them to acquire self-control. Anyone having acquired the faculty of following high principles and ideals, while putting into the background all personal predilection; anyone capable of always performing his duty, even though inclinations and sympathies would like to seduce him from this duty—such a person is unconsciously an initiate in the midst of ordinary life. He will need but little to succeed in this particular trial. Indeed, a certain

88

measure of initiation thus unconsciously acquired in life will, as a rule, be indispensable for success in this second trial. For even as it is difficult for those who have not learned to spell correctly in their childhood to make good this deficiency when fully grown up, so too it is difficult to develop the necessary degree of self-control at the moment of looking into the higher worlds, if this ability has not been acquired to a certain degree in ordinary life. The objects of the physical world do not alter, whatever the nature of our wishes, desires, and inclinations. In the higher worlds, however, our wishes, desires, and inclinations are causes that produce effects. If we wish to produce a particular effect in these worlds, we must hold ourselves completely under control; we must strictly follow the right rules and subdue every arbitrary impulse.

One human quality is of very special importance at this stage of initiation, namely, an *unquestionably sound judgment*. Attention should be paid to the training of this faculty during all the previous stages; for it now remains to be proved whether the candidate is shaping in a way that shows him to be fit for the true path of knowledge. Further progress is now only possible if he is able to distinguish illusion, superstition, and everything fantastic, from true reality. This is, at first, more difficult to accomplish in the higher stages of existence than in the lower. Every prejudice, every cherished opinion with regard to the things in question, must vanish; truth alone must guide. There must be perfect readiness to abandon at once any idea, opinion, or inclination when logical thought demands it. Certainty in higher worlds is only likely to be attained when personal opinion is never considered.

People whose mode of thought tends to fancifulness and superstition can never make progress on the path to higher knowledge. It is indeed a precious treasure that the student is to acquire. All doubt regarding the higher worlds is removed from him. With all their laws they reveal themselves to his gaze. But he cannot acquire this treasure so long as he is the prey of fancies and illusions. It would indeed be fatal if his imagination and his prejudices ran away with his intellect. Dreamers and fantastical people are as unfit for the path to higher knowledge as superstitious people. This cannot be over-emphasized. For the most dangerous enemies on the way to knowledge of the higher worlds lurk in such fantastical reveries and superstitions. Yet no one need believe that the student loses all sense of poetry in life, all power of enthusiasm because the words: *You must be rid of all prejudice,* are written over the portal leading to the second trial of initiation, and because over the portal at the entrance to the first trial he read: *Without normal common sense all thine efforts are in vain.*

If the candidate is in this way sufficiently advanced, a third trial awaits him. He finds here no definite goal to be reached. All is left in his own hands. He finds himself in a situation where nothing impels him to act. He must find his way all alone and out of himself. Things or people to stimulate him to action are non-existent. Nothing and nobody can give him the strength he needs but he himself alone. Failure to find this inner strength will leave him standing where he was. Few of those, however, who have successfully passed the previous trials will fail to find the necessary strength at this point. Either they will have turned back already or they succeed at this point also. All that the candidate requires is the ability to come quickly to terms with himself, for he must here find his *higher self* in the truest sense of the word. He must rapidly decide in all things to listen to the inspiration of the spirit. There is no time for doubt or hesitation. Every moment of hesitation would prove that he was still unfit. Whatever prevents him from listening to the voice of the spirit must be courageously overcome. It is a question of showing presence of mind in this situation, and the training at this stage is concerned with the perfect development of this quality. All the accustomed inducements to act or even to think now cease. In order not to remain inactive he must not lose himself, for only within himself can he find the one central point of vantage where he can gain a firm hold. No one on reading this, without further acquaintance with these matters, should feel an antipathy for this principle of being thrown back on oneself, for success in this trial brings with it a moment of supreme happiness.

At this stage, no less than at the others, ordinary life is itself an esoteric training for many. For anyone having reached the point of being able, when suddenly confronted with some task

92

or problem in life, to come to a swift decision without hesitation or delay, for him life itself has been a training in this sense. Such situations are here meant in which success is instantly lost if action is not rapid. A person who is quick to act when a misfortune is imminent, whereas a few moments of hesitation would have seen the misfortune an accomplished fact, and who has turned this ability into a permanent personal quality, has unconsciously acquired the degree of maturity necessary for the third trial. For at this stage everything centers round the development of absolute presence of mind. This trial is known as the *Air-Trial*, because while undergoing it the candidate can support himself neither upon the firm basis of external incentive nor upon the figures, tones, and colors which he has learned at the stages of *preparation* and *enlightenment*, but exclusively upon himself.

Upon successfully passing this trial the student is permitted to enter the *temple of higher wisdom*. All that is here said on this subject can only be the slenderest allusion. The task now to be performed is often expressed in the statement that the student must take an oath never to betray anything he has learned. These expressions, however, "oath" and "betray", are inappropriate and actually misleading. There is no question of an oath in the ordinary sense of the word, but rather of an experience that comes at this stage of development. The candidate learns how to apply the higher knowledge, how to place it at the service of humanity. He then begins really and truly to understand the world. It is not so much a question of withholding the higher truths, but far more of serving them in the right way and with the necessary tact. The silence he is to keep refers to something quite different. He acquires this fine quality with regard to things he had previously spoken, and especially with regard to the manner in which they were spoken. He would be a poor initiate who did not place all the higher knowledge he had acquired at the service of humanity, as well and as far as this is possible. The only obstacle to giving information in these matters is the lack of understanding on the part of the recipients. It is true, of course, that the higher knowledge does not lend itself to promiscuous talk; but no one having reached the stage of development described above is actually forbidden

94

to say anything. No other person, no being exacts an oath from him with this intent. Everything is left to his own responsibility, and he learns in every situation to discover within himself what he has to do, and an oath means nothing more than that he has been found qualified to be entrusted with such a responsibility.

If the candidate is found fit for the foregoing experiences, he is then given what is called symbolically the *draught of forgetfulness*. This means that he is initiated into the secret knowledge that enables him to act without being continually disturbed by the lower memory. This is necessary for the initiate, for he must have full faith in the immediate present. He must be able to destroy the veil of memory which envelops man every moment of his life. If we judge something that happens to us today according to the experience of yesterday, we are exposed to a multitude of errors. Of course this does not mean that experience gained in life should be renounced. It should always be kept in mind as clearly as possible. But the initiate must have the ability to judge every new experience wholly according to what is inherent in it, and let it react upon him, unobscured by the past. We must be prepared at every moment that every object and every being can bring to us some new revelation. If we judge the new by the standard of the old we are liable to error. The memory of past experiences will be of greatest use for the very reason that it enables us to perceive the new. Had we not gone through a definite experience we should perhaps be blind to the qualities of the object or being that comes before us. Thus experience should serve the purpose of perceiving the new and not of judging it by the standard of the old. In this respect the initiate acquires certain definite qualities, and thereby many things are revealed to him which remain concealed from the uninitiated.

The second draught presented to the initiate is the *draught of remembrance*. Through its agency he acquires the faculty of retaining the knowledge of the higher truths ever present in his soul. Ordinary memory would be unequal to this task. We must unite ourselves and become as one with the higher truths. We must not only know them, but be able, quite as a matter of course, to manifest and administer them in living actions, even as we ordinarily eat and drink.

They must become our practice, our habit, our inclination. There must be no need to keep thinking about them in the ordinary sense; they must come to living expression through man himself; they must flow through him as the functions of life through his organism. *Thus doth man ever raise himself, in a spiritual sense, to that same stature to which nature raised him in a physical sense.*

IV

SOME PRACTICAL ASPECTS

T HE training of thoughts and feelings, pursued in the way described in the chapters on *Preparation, Enlightenment,* and *Initiation,* introduces into the soul and spirit the same organic symmetry with which nature has constructed the physical body. Before this development, soul and spirit are undifferentiated masses. The clairvoyant perceives them as interlacing, rotating, cloud-like spirals, dully glimmering in reddish, reddish-brown, or reddish-yellow tones. After this training they begin to assume a brilliant yellowish-green, or greenish-blue color, and show a regular structure. This inner regularity, leading to higher knowledge, is attained when the student introduces into his thoughts and feelings the same orderly system with which nature

98

has endowed his bodily organs that enable him to see, hear, digest, breathe, speak. Gradually he learns to breathe and see with his soul, to speak and hear with the spirit.

In the following pages some practical aspects of the higher education of soul and spirit will be treated in greater detail. They are such that anyone can put them into practice regardless of other rules, and thereby be led some distance further into spiritual science.

A particular effort must be made to cultivate the quality of patience. Every symptom of impatience produces a paralyzing, even a destructive effect on the higher faculties that slumber in us. We must not expect an immeasurable view into the higher worlds from one day to the next, for we should assuredly be disappointed. Contentment with the smallest fragment attained, repose and tranquillity, must more and more take possession of the soul. It is quite understandable that the student should await results with impatience; but he will achieve nothing so long as he fails to master this impatience. Nor is it of any use to combat this impatience merely in the ordinary sense, for it will become only that much stronger. We over-

99

look it in self-deception while it plants itself all the more firmly in the depths of the soul. It is only when we ever and again surrender ourselves to a certain definite thought, making it absolutely our own, that any result can be attained. This thought is as follows: *I must certainly do everything I can for the training and development of my soul and spirit, but I shall wait patiently until higher powers shall have found me worthy of definite enlightenment.* If this thought becomes so powerful in the student that it grows into an actual feature of his character, he is treading the right path. This feature soon sets its mark on his exterior. The gaze of his eye becomes steady, the movement of his body becomes sure, his decisions definite, and all that goes under the name of nervousness gradually disappears. Rules that appear trifling and insignificant must be taken into account. For example, supposing someone affronts us. Before our training we should have directed our resentment against the offender; a wave of anger would have surged up within us. In a similar case, however, the thought is immediately present in the mind of the student that such an affront makes no difference to his intrinsic worth. And he does whatever must be done to meet the affront with calm and composure, and not in a spirit of anger. Of course it is not a case of simply accepting every affront, but of acting with the same calm composure when dealing with an affront against our own person as we would if the affront were directed against another person, in whose favor we had the right to intervene. It must always be remembered that this training is not carried out in crude outward processes, but in subtle, silent alterations in the life of thought and feeling.

Patience has the effect of attraction, impatience the effect of repulsion on the treasures of higher knowledge. In the higher regions of existence nothing can be attained by haste and unrest. Above all things, desire and craving must be silenced, for these are qualities of the soul before which all higher knowledge shyly withdraws. However precious this knowledge is accounted, the student must not crave it if he wishes to attain it. If he wishes to have it for his own sake, he will never attain it. This requires him to be honest with himself in his innermost soul. He must in no case be under any illusion concerning his own self. With a feeling of inner truth he must look his own faults, weaknesses, and unfitness full in the face. The moment he tries to excuse to himself any one of his weaknesses, he has placed a stone in his way on the path which is to lead him upward. Such obstacles can only be removed by self-enlightenment. There is only one way to get rid of faults and failings, and that is by a clear recognition of them. Everything slumbers in the human soul and can be awakened. A person can even improve his intellect and reason, if he quietly and calmly makes it clear to himself why he is weak in this respect. Such self-knowledge is, of course, difficult, for the temptation to self-deception is immeasurably great. Anyone making a habit of being truthful with himself opens the portal leading to a deeper insight.

All curiosity must fall away from the student. He must rid himself as much as possible of the habit of asking questions merely for the sake of gratifying a selfish thirst for knowledge. He must only ask when knowledge can serve to perfect his own being in the service of evolution. Nevertheless, his delight in knowledge and his devotion to it should in no way be hampered. He should listen devoutly to all that contributes to such an end, and should seek every opportunity for such devotional attention.

Special attention must be paid in esoteric training to the education of the life of desires. This does not mean that we are to become free of desire, for if we are to attain something we must also desire it, and desire will always tend to fulfillment if backed by a particular force. This force is derived from a right knowledge. *Do not desire at all until you know what is right in any one sphere.* That is one of the golden rules for the student. The wise man first ascertains the laws of the world, and then his desires become powers which realize themselves. The following example brings this out clearly. There are certainly many people who would like to learn from their own observation something about their life before birth. Such a desire is altogether useless and leads to no result, so long as the person in question has not acquired a knowledge of the laws that govern the nature of the eternal, a knowledge of these laws in their subtlest and most intimate character, through the study of spiritual science. But if, having really acquired this knowledge, he wishes to proceed further, his desire, now ennobled and purified, will enable him to do so.

It is also no use saying: I particularly wish to examine my previous life, and shall study only for this purpose. We must rather be capable of abandoning this desire, of eliminating it altogether, and of studying, at first, with no such intention. We should cultivate a feeling of joy and devotion for what we learn, with no thought of the above end in view. We should learn to cherish and foster a particular desire in such a way that it brings with it its own fulfillment.

If we become angered, vexed or annoyed, we erect a wall around ourselves in the soul-world, and the forces which are to develop the eyes of the soul cannot approach. For instance, if a person angers me he sends forth a psychic current into the soul-world. I cannot see this current as long as I am myself capable of anger. My own anger conceals it from me. We must not, however, suppose that when we are free from anger we shall immediately have a psychic (astral) vision. For this purpose an organ of vision must have been developed in the soul. The beginnings

104

of such an organ are latent in every human being, but remain ineffective as long as he is capable of anger. Yet this organ is not immediately present the moment anger has been combated to a small extent. We must rather persevere in this combating of anger and proceed patiently on our way; then some day we shall find that this eye of the soul has become developed. Of course, anger is not the only failing to be combated for the attainment of this end. Many grow impatient or sceptical, because they have for years combated certain qualities, and yet clairvoyance has not ensued. In that case they have just trained some qualities and allowed others to run riot. The gift of clairvoyance only manifests itself when all those qualities which stunt the growth of the latent faculties are suppressed. Undoubtedly, the beginnings of such seeing and hearing may appear at an earlier period, but these are only young and tender shoots which are subjected to all possible error, and which, if not carefully tended and guarded, may quickly die.

Other qualities which, like anger and vexation, have to be combated, are timidity, superstition, prejudice, vanity and ambition, curiosity, the

105

mania for imparting information, and the making of distinctions in human beings according to the outward characteristics of rank, sex, race, and so forth. In our time it is difficult for people to understand how the combating of such qualities can have anything to do with the heightening of the faculty of cognition. But every spiritual scientist knows that much more depends upon such matters than upon the increase of intelligence and the employment of artificial exercises. Especially can misunderstanding arise if we believe that we must become foolhardy in order to be fearless; that we must close our eyes to the differences between people, because we must combat the prejudices of rank, race, and so forth. Rather is it true that a correct estimate of all things is to be attained only when we are no longer entangled in prejudice. Even in the ordinary sense it is true that the fear of some phenomenon prevents us from estimating it rightly; that a racial prejudice prevents us from seeing into a man's soul. It is this ordinary sense that the student must develop in all its delicacy and subtlety.

Every word spoken without having been thoroughly purged in thought is a stone thrown in the way of esoteric training. And here something must be considered which can only be explained by giving an example. If anything be said to which we must reply, we must be careful to consider the speaker's opinion, feeling, and even his prejudice, rather than what we ourselves have to say at the moment on the subject under discussion. In this example a refined quality of tact is indicated, to the cultivation of which the student must devote his care. He must learn to judge what importance it may have for the other person if he opposes the latter's opinion with his own. This does not mean that he must withhold his opinion. There can be no question of that. But he must listen to the speaker as carefully and as attentively as he possibly can and let his reply derive its form from what he has just heard. In such cases one particular thought recurs ever and again to the student, and he is treading the right path if this thought lives with him to the extent of becoming a trait of his character. This thought is as follows: *The importance lies not in the difference of our opinions but in his discovering through his own effort what is right if I contribute something toward it.* Thoughts of this and of a similar nature cause the character and the behavior of the student to be permeated with a quality of gentleness, which is one of the chief means used in all esoteric training. Harshness scares away the soul-pictures that should open the eye of the soul; gentleness clears the obstacles away and unseals the inner organs.

Along with gentleness, another quality will presently be developed in the soul of the student: that of quietly paying attention to all the subtleties in the soul-life of his environment, while reducing to absolute silence any activity within his own soul. The soul-life of his environment will impress itself on him in such a way that his own soul will grow, and as it grows, become regular in its structure, as a plant expanding in the sunlight. Gentleness and patient reserve open the soul to the soul-world and the spirit to the spirit-world. Persevere in silent inner seclusion; close the senses to all that they brought you before your training; reduce to absolute immobility all the thoughts which, according to your previous habits, surged within you; become quite still and silent within, wait in patience, and then the higher worlds will begin to fashion and perfect the organs of sight and hearing in your soul and spirit. Do not expect immediately to see and hear in the world of soul and spirit, for all that you are doing does but contribute to the development of your higher senses, and you will only be able to hear with soul and spirit when you possess these higher senses. Having persevered for a time in silent inner seclusion, go about your customary daily affairs, imprinting deeply upon your mind this thought: *"Some day, when I have grown sufficiently, I shall attain that which I am destined to attain,"* and make no attempt to attract forcefully any of these higher powers to yourself. Every student receives these instructions at the outset. By observing them he perfects himself. If he neglects them, all his labor is in vain. But they are only difficult of achievement for the impatient and the unpersevering. No other obstacles exist save those which we ourselves place in our own path, and which can be avoided by all who really will. This point must be continually emphasized, because many people form an altogether wrong conception of the difficulties that beset the path to higher knowledge. It is easier, in a certain sense, to accomplish the first steps along this path than to get the better of the commonest every-day difficulties without this training. Apart from this, only such things are here imparted as are attended by no danger whatsoever to the health of soul and body. There are other ways which lead more quickly to the goal, but what is here explained has nothing to do with them, because they have certain effects which no experienced spiritual scientist considers desirable. Since fragmentary information concerning these ways is continually finding its way into publicity, express warning must be given against entering upon them. For reasons which only the initiated can understand, these ways can never be made public in their true form. The fragments appearing here and there can never lead to profitable results, but may easily undermine health, happiness, and peace of mind. It would be far better for people to avoid having anything to do with such things than to risk entrusting themselves to wholly dark forces, of whose nature and origin they can know nothing.

Something may here be said concerning the environment in which this training should be undertaken, for this is not without some importance. And yet the case differs for almost every person.

Anyone practicing in an environment filled only with self-seeking interests, as for example, the modern struggle for existence, must be conscious of the fact that these interests are not without their effect on the development of his spiritual organs. It is true that the inner laws of these organs are so powerful that this influence cannot be fatally injurious. Just as a lily can never grow into a thistle, however inappropriate its environment, so, too, the eye of the soul can never grow to anything but its destined shape even though it be subjected to the self-seeking interests of modern cities. But under all circumstances it is well if the student seeks, now and again, his environment in the restful peace, the inner dignity and sweetness of nature. Especially fortunate is the student who can carry out his esoteric training surrounded by the green world of plants, or among the sunny hills, where nature weaves her web of sweet simplicity. This environment develops the inner organs in a harmony which can never ensue in a modern city. More favorably situated than the townsman is the person who, during his childhood at least, had been able to breathe the fragrance of pines, to gaze on snowy peaks, and observe the silent activity of woodland creatures and insects. Yet no city-dweller should fail to give to the organs of his soul and spirit, as they develop, the nurture that comes from the inspired teachings of spiritual research. If our eyes cannot follow the woods in their mantel of green every spring, day by day, we should instead open our soul to the glorious teachings of the Bhagavad Gita, or of St. John's Gospel, or of St. Thomas à Kempis, and to the descriptions resulting from spiritual science. There are many ways to the summit of insight, but much depends on the right choice. The spiritually experienced could say much concerning these paths, much that might seem strange to the uninitiated. Someone, for instance, might be very far advanced on the path; he might be standing, so to speak, at the very entrance of sight and hearing with soul and spirit; he is then fortunate enough to make a journey over the calm or maybe tempestuous ocean, and a veil falls away from the eyes of his soul: suddenly he becomes a seer. Another is also so far advanced that this veil only needs to be loosened; this occurs through some stroke of destiny. On another this stroke might well have had the effect of paralyzing his powers and undermining his energy; for the esoteric student it becomes the occasion of his *enlightenment*. A third perseveres patiently for years without any marked result. Suddenly, while silently seated in his quiet chamber, spiritual light envelops him; the walls disappear, become transparent for his soul, and a new world expands before his eyes that have become seeing, or resounds in his ears that have become spiritually hearing.

V

THE CONDITIONS OF
ESOTERIC TRAINING

THE conditions attached to esoteric training are not arbitrary. They are the natural
outcome of esoteric knowledge. Just as no one
can become a painter who refuses to handle a
paint-brush, so, too, no one can receive esoteric
training who is unwilling to meet the demands
considered necessary by the teacher. In the
main, the latter can give nothing but advice,
and everything he says should be accepted in this
sense. He has already passed through the preparatory stages leading to a knowledge of the
higher worlds, and knows from experience what
is necessary. It depends entirely upon the free-will
of each individual human being whether or not
he choose to tread the same path. To insist on being admitted to esoteric training without fulfilling

114

the conditions would be equivalent to saying: "Teach me how to paint, but do not ask me to handle a paint-brush." The teacher can never offer anything unless the recipient comes forward to meet him of his own free-will. But it must be emphasized that a general desire for higher knowledge is not sufficient. This desire will, of course, be felt by many, but nothing can be achieved by it alone so long as the special conditions attached to esoteric training are not accepted. This point should be considered by those who complain that the training is difficult. Failure or unwillingness to fulfill these strict conditions must entail the abandonment of esoteric training, for the time being. It is true, the conditions are strict, yet they are not harsh, since their fulfillment not only should be, but indeed must be a voluntary action.

If this fact be overlooked, esoteric training can easily appear in the light of a coercion of the soul or the conscience; for the training is based on the development of the inner life, and the teacher must necessarily give advice concerning this inner life. But there is no question of compulsion when a demand is met out of free choice. To ask of the teacher: "Give me your higher knowledge, but leave me my customary emotions, feelings, and thoughts," would be an impossible demand. In this case the gratification of curiosity and desire for knowledge would be the only motive. When pursued in such a spirit, however, higher knowledge can never be attained.

Let us now consider in turn the conditions imposed on the student. It should be emphasized that the complete fulfillment of any one of these conditions is not insisted upon, but only the corresponding effort. No one can wholly fulfill them, but everyone can start on the path toward them. It is the effort of will that matters, and the ready disposition to enter upon this path.

1. *The first condition is that the student should pay heed to the advancement of bodily and spiritual health.* Of course, health does not depend, in the first instance, upon the individual; but the effort to improve in this respect lies within the scope of all. Sound knowledge can alone proceed from sound human beings. The unhealthy are not rejected, but it is demanded of the student that he should have the will to lead a healthy life. In this respect he must attain the greatest possible in-

116

dependence. The good counsels of others, freely bestowed though generally unsought, are as a rule superfluous. Each must endeavor to take care of himself. From the physical aspect it will be more a question of warding off harmful influences than of anything else. In fulfilling our duties we must often do things that are detrimental to our health. We must decide at the right moment to place duty higher than the care of our health. But just think how much can be avoided with a little good will. Duty must in many cases stand higher than health, often, even, than life itself; but pleasure must never stand higher, as far as the student is concerned. For him pleasure can only be a means to health and to life, and in this connection we must, above all, be honest and truthful with ourselves. There is no use in leading an ascetic life when the underlying motive is the same in this case as in other enjoyments. Some may derive satisfaction from asceticism just as others can from wine-bibbing, but they must not imagine that this sort of asceticism will assist them in attaining higher knowledge. Many ascribe to their circumstances everything which apparently prevents them from making progress. They say they

117

cannot develop themselves under their conditions of life. Now, many may find it desirable for other reasons to change their conditions of life, but no one need do so for the purpose of esoteric training. For the latter, a person need only do as much as possible, whatever his position, to further the health of body and soul. Every kind of work can serve the whole of humanity; and it is a surer sign of greatness of soul to perceive clearly how necessary for this whole is a petty, perhaps even an offensive employment than to think: "This work is not good enough for me; I am destined for something better." Of special importance for the student is the striving for complete health of mind. An unhealthy life of thought and feeling will not fail to obstruct the path to higher knowledge. Clear, calm thinking, with stability of feeling and emotion, form here the basis of all work. Nothing should be further removed from the student than an inclination toward a fantastical, excitable life, toward nervousness, exaggeration, and fanaticism. He should acquire a healthy outlook on all circumstances of life; he should meet the demands of life with steady assurance, quietly letting all things make their impression on him

118

and reveal their message. He should be at pains to do justice to life on every occasion. All one-sided and extravagant tendencies in his sentiments and criticisms should be avoided. Failing this, he would find his way merely into worlds of his own imagination, instead of higher worlds; in place of truth, his own pet opinions would assert themselves. It is better for the student to be matter-of-fact, than excitable and fantastic.

2. *The second condition is that the student should feel himself co-ordinated as a link in the whole of life.* Much is included in the fulfillment of this condition, but each can only fulfill it in his own manner. If I am a teacher, and my pupil does not fulfill my expectations, I must not direct my resentment against him but against myself. I must feel myself as one with my pupil, to the extent of asking myself: "Is my pupil's deficiency not the result of my own action?" Instead of directing my feelings against him I shall rather reflect on my own attitude, so that the pupil may in the future be better able to satisfy my demands. Proceeding from such an attitude, a change will come over the student's whole way of thinking. This holds good in all things, great or small. Such

an attitude of mind, for instance, alters the way I regard a criminal. I suspend my judgment and say to myself: "I am, like him, only a human being. Through favorable circumstances I received an education which perhaps alone saved me from a similar fate." I may then also come to the conclusion that this human brother of mine would have become a different man had my teachers taken the same pains with him they took with me. I shall reflect on the fact that something was given to me which was withheld from him, that I enjoy my fortune precisely because it was denied him. And then I shall naturally come to think of myself as a link in the whole of humanity and a sharer in the responsibility for everything that occurs. This does not imply that such a thought should be immediately translated into external acts of agitation. It should be cherished in stillness within the soul. Then quite gradually it will set its mark on the outward demeanor of the student. In such matters each can only begin by reforming himself. It is of no avail, in the sense of the foregoing thoughts, to make general demands on the whole of humanity. It is easy to decide what men ought to be; but the student works in the depths, not on the surface. It would therefore be quite wrong to relate the demand here indicated with any external, least of all political, demands; with such matters this training can have nothing to do. Political agitators know, as a rule, what to demand of other people; but they say little of demands on themselves.

3. This brings us to *the third condition. The student must work his way upward to the realization that his thoughts and feelings are as important for the world as his actions. It must be realized that it is equally injurious to hate a fellow-being as to strike him.* The realization will then follow that by perfecting ourselves we accomplish something not only for ourselves, but for the whole world. The world derives equal benefit from our untainted feelings and thoughts as from our good demeanor, and as long as we cannot believe in this cosmic importance of our inner life, we are unfit for the path that is here described. We are only filled with the right faith in the significance of our inner self, of our soul, when we work at it as though it were at least as real as all external things. We must admit that

our every feeling produces an effect, just as does every action of our hand.

4. These words already express *the fourth condition: to acquire the conviction that the real being of man does not lie in his exterior but in his interior.* Anyone regarding himself as a product of the outer world, as a result of the physical world, cannot succeed in this esoteric training, for the feeling that we are beings of soul and spirit forms its very basis. The acquisition of this feeling renders the student fit to distinguish between inner duty and outward success. He learns that the one cannot be directly measured by the other. He must find the proper mean between what is indicated by external conditions and what he recognizes as the right conduct for himself. He should not force upon his environment anything for which it can have no understanding, but also he must be quite free from the desire to do only what can be appreciated by those around him. The voice of his own soul struggling honestly toward knowledge must bring him the one and only recognition of the truths for which he stands. But he must learn as much as he possibly can from his environment so

as to discover what those around him need, and what is good for them. In this way he will develop within himself what is known in spiritual science as the "spiritual balance". An open heart for the needs of the outer world lies on one of the scales, and inner fortitude and unfaltering endurance on the other.

5. This brings us to *the fifth condition: steadfastness in carrying out a resolution.* Nothing should induce the student to deviate from a resolution he may have taken, save only the perception that he was in error. Every resolution is a force, and if this force does not produce an immediate effect at the point to which it was applied, it works nevertheless on in its own way. Success is only decisive when an action arises from desire. But all actions arising from desire are worthless in relation to the higher worlds. There, love for an action is alone the decisive factor. In this love, every impulse that impels the student to action should fulfill itself. Undismayed by failure, he will never grow weary of endeavoring repeatedly to translate some resolution into action. And in this way he reaches the stage of not waiting to see the outward effect of his actions, but of con-

tenting himself with performing them. He will learn to sacrifice his actions, even his whole being, to the world, however the world may receive his sacrifice. Readiness for a sacrifice, for an offering such as this, must be shown by all who would pursue the path of esoteric training.

6. *A sixth condition is the development of a feeling of thankfulness for everything with which man is favored.* We must realize that our existence is a gift from the entire universe. How much is needed to enable each one of us to receive and maintain his existence! How much do we not owe to nature and to our fellow human beings! Thoughts such as these must come naturally to all who seek esoteric training, for if the latter do not feel inclined to entertain them, they will be incapable of developing within themselves that all-embracing love which is necessary for the attainment of higher knowledge. Nothing can reveal itself to us which we do not love. And every revelation must fill us with thankfulness, for we ourselves are the richer for it.

7. *All these conditions must be united in a seventh: to regard life unceasingly in the manner demanded by these conditions.* The student

124

thus makes it possible to give his life the stamp of uniformity. All his modes of expression will, in this way, be brought into harmony, and no longer contradict each other. And thus he will prepare himself for the inner tranquillity he must attain during the preliminary steps of his training.

Anyone sincerely showing the good will to fulfill these conditions may decide to seek esoteric training. He will then be ready to follow the advice given above. Much of this advice may appear to be merely on the surface, and many will perhaps say that they did not expect the training to proceed in such strict forms. But everything interior must manifest itself in an exterior way, and just as a picture is not evident when it exists only in the mind of the painter, so, too, there can be no esoteric training without outward expression. Disregard for strict forms is only shown by those who do not know that the exterior is the avenue of expression for the interior. No doubt it is the spirit that really matters, and not the form; but just as form without spirit is null and void, so also would spirit remain inactive if it did not create for itself a form.

The above conditions are calculated to render the student strong enough to fulfill the further demands made on him during his training. If he fail in these conditions he will hesitate before each new demand, and without them he will lack that faith in man which he must possess. For all striving for truth must be founded on faith in and true love for man. But though this is the foundation it is not the source of all striving for truth, for such striving can only flow from the soul's own fountain-head of strength. And the love of man must gradually widen to a love for all living creatures, yes, for all existence. Through failure to fulfill the condition here given, the student will lack the perfect love for everything that fashions and creates, and the inclination to refrain from all destruction as such. He must so train himself that not only in his actions but also in his words, feelings, and thoughts he will never destroy anything for the sake of destruction. His joy must be in growth and life, and he must only lend his hand to destruction, when he is also able, through and by means of destruction, to promote new life. This does not mean that the student must simply look on while evil runs riot, but rather that he must seek even in evil that side through which he may transform it into good. He will then see more and more clearly that evil and imperfection may best be combated by the creation of the good and the perfect. The student knows that out of nothing, nothing can be created, but also that the imperfect can be transformed into the perfect. Anyone developing within himself the disposition to create, will soon find himself capable of facing evil in the right way.

It must be clearly realized that the purpose of this training is to build and not to destroy. The student should therefore bring with him the good will for sincere and devoted work, and not the intention to criticize and destroy. He should be capable of devotion, for he must learn what he does not yet know; he should look reverently on that which discloses itself. Work and devotion, these are the fundamental qualities which must be demanded of the student. Some come to realize that they are making no progress, though in their own opinion they are untiringly active. The reason is that they have not grasped the meaning of work and devotion in the right way. Work done for the sake of success will be the least successful, and learning pursued without devotion will be the least conducive to progress. Only the love of work, and not of success, leads to progress. And if in learning the student seeks straight thinking and sound judgment, he need not stunt his devotion by doubts and suspicions.

We are not reduced to servile subjection in listening to some information with quiet devotion and because we do not at once oppose it with our own opinion. Anyone having advanced some way in the attainment of higher knowledge knows that he owes everything to quiet attention and active reflection, and not to wilful personal judgment. We should always bear in mind that we do not need to learn what we are already able to judge. Therefore if our sole intention is to judge, we can learn nothing more. Esoteric training, however, centers in learning; we must have absolutely the good will to be learners. If we cannot understand something, it is far better not to judge than to judge adversely. We can wait until later for a true understanding. The higher we climb the ladder of knowledge, the more do we require the faculty of listening with quiet devotion. All perception of truth, all life and activity in the world of the spirit, become subtle and delicate in comparison with the processes of the ordinary intellect and of life in the physical world. The more the sphere of our activity widens out before us, the more delicate are the processes in which we are engaged. It is for this reason that men arrive at such different opinions and points of view regarding the higher regions. But there is one and only one opinion regarding higher truths and this one opinion is within reach of all who, through work and devotion, have so risen that they can really behold truth and contemplate it. Opinions differing from the one true opinion can only be arrived at when people, insufficiently prepared, judge in accordance with their pet theories, their habitual ways of thought, and so forth. Just as there is only one correct opinion concerning a mathematical problem, so also is this true with regard to the higher worlds. But before such an opinion can be reached, due preparation must first be undergone. If this were only considered, the conditions attached to esoteric training would be surprising to none. It is indeed true that truth and the higher life abide in every soul, and that each can and must find them for himself. But they lie deeply buried, and can only be brought up from their deep shafts after all obstacles have been cleared away. Only the experienced can advise how this may be done. Such advice is found in spiritual science. No truth is forced on anyone; no dogma is proclaimed; a way only is pointed out. It is true that everyone could find this way unaided, but only perhaps after many incarnations. By esoteric training this way is shortened. We thus reach more quickly a point from which we can co-operate in those worlds where the salvation and evolution of man are furthered by spiritual work.

This brings to an end the indications to be given in connection with the attainment of knowledge of the higher worlds. In the following chapter, and in further connection with the above, it will be shown how this development affects the higher elements of the human organism (the soul-organism or astral body, and the spirit or thought-body). In this way the indications here given will be placed in a new light, and it will be possible to penetrate them in a deeper sense.

VI

SOME RESULTS OF INITIATION

ONE of the fundamental principles of true
spiritual science is that the one who devotes
himself to its study should do so with full consciousness; he should attempt nothing and practice nothing without knowledge of the effect produced. A teacher of spiritual science who gives
advice or instruction will, at the same time, always explain to those striving for higher knowledge the effects produced on body, soul, and spirit,
if his advice and instructions be followed.

Some effects produced upon the soul of the
student will here be indicated. For only those
who know such things as they are here communicated can undertake in full consciousness the
exercises that lead to knowledge of the higher
worlds. Without the latter no genuine esoteric

131

training is possible, for it must be understood that all groping in the dark is discouraged, and that failure to pursue this training with open eyes may lead to mediumship, but not to exact clairvoyance in the sense of spiritual science.

The exercises described in the preceding chapters, if practiced in the right way, involve certain changes in the organism of the soul (astral body). The latter is only perceptible to the clairvoyant, and may be compared to a cloud, psycho-spiritually luminous to a certain degree, in the center of which the physical body is discernible. (A description will be found in the author's book, *Theosophy*.) In this astral body desires, lusts, passions, and ideas become visible in a spiritual way. Sensual appetites, for instance, create the impression of a dark red radiance with a definite shape; a pure and noble thought finds its expression in a reddish-violet radiance; the clear-cut concept of the logical thinker is experienced as a yellowish figure with sharply defined outline; the confused thought of the muddled head appears as a figure with vague outline. The thoughts of a person with one-sided, queer views appear sharply outlined but immobile, while the

132

thoughts of people accessible to the points of view of others are seen to have mobile, change-able outlines. (In all these and the following de-scriptions it must be noted that by seeing a color, spiritual seeing is meant. When the clairvoyant speaks of "seeing red", he means: "I have an ex-perience, in a psycho-spiritual way, which is equivalent to the physical experience when an impression of red is received." This mode of expression is here used because it is perfectly natural to the clairvoyant. If this point is over-looked, a mere color-vision may easily be mis-taken for a genuine clairvoyant experience.)

The further the student advances in his inner development, the more regular will be the differ-entiation within his astral body. The latter is con-fused and undifferentiated in the case of a person of undeveloped inner life; yet the clairvoyant can perceive even the unorganized astral body as a figure standing out distinctly from its environ-ment. It extends from the center of the head to the middle of the physical body, and appears like an independent body possessing certain organs. The organs now to be considered are perceptible to the clairvoyant near the following parts of the physical body: the first between the eyes; the second near the larynx; the third in the region of the heart; the fourth in the so-called pit of the stomach; the fifth and sixth are situated in the abdomen. These organs are technically known as wheels, *chakrams,* or lotus flowers. They are so called on account of their likeness to wheels or flowers, but of course it should be clearly understood that such an expression is not to be applied more literally than is the term "wings" when referring to the two halves of the lungs. Just as there is no question of wings in the case of the lungs, so, too, in the case of the lotus flowers the expression must be taken figuratively. In undeveloped persons these lotus flowers are dark in color, motionless and inert. In the clairvoyant, however, they are luminous, mobile, and of variegated color. Something of this kind applies to the medium, though in a different way; this question, however, need not be pursued here any further.

Now, when the student begins his exercises, the lotus flowers become more luminous; later on they begin to revolve. When this occurs,

134

clairvoyance begins. For these flowers are the sense-organs of the soul, and their revolutions express the fact that the clairvoyant perceives supersensibly. What was said previously concerning spiritual seeing applies equally to these revolutions and even to the lotus flowers themselves. No one can perceive the supersensible until he has developed his astral senses in this way. Thanks to the spiritual organ situated in the vicinity of the larynx, it becomes possible to survey clairvoyantly the thoughts and mentality of other beings, and to obtain a deeper insight into the true laws of natural phenomena. The organ situated near the heart permits of clairvoyant knowledge of the sentiments and disposition of other souls. When developed, this organ also makes it possible to observe certain deeper forces in animals and plants. By means of the organ in the so-called pit of the stomach, knowledge is acquired of the talents and capacities of souls; by its means, too, the part played by animals, plants, stones, metals, atmospheric phenomena and so on in the household of nature becomes apparent.

The organ in the vicinity of the larynx has

135

sixteen petals or spokes; the one in the region of the heart twelve, and the one in the pit of the stomach ten.

Now certain activities of the soul are connected with the development of these organs, and anyone devoting himself to them in a certain definite way contributes something to the development of the corresponding organs. In the sixteen-petalled lotus, eight of its sixteen petals were developed in the remote past during an earlier stage of human evolution. Man himself contributed nothing to this development; he received them as a gift from nature, at a time when his consciousness was in a dull, dreamy condition. At that stage of human evolution they were in active use, but the manner of their activity was only compatible with that dull state of consciousness. As consciousness became clearer and brighter, the petals became obscured and ceased their activity. Man himself can now develop the remaining eight petals by means of conscious exercises, and thereby the whole lotus flower becomes luminous and mobile. The acquisition of certain faculties depends on the development of each one of the sixteen petals. Yet, as already shown, only

136

eight can be consciously developed; the remainder then appear of their own accord.

The development proceeds in the following manner. The student must first apply himself with care and attention to certain functions of the soul hitherto exercised by him in a careless and inattentive manner. *There are eight such functions. The first is the way in which ideas and conceptions are acquired.* In this respect people usually allow themselves to be led by chance alone. They see or hear one thing or another and form their ideas accordingly. As long as this is the case the sixteen petals of the lotus flower remain ineffective. It is only when the student begins to take his self-education in hand, in this respect, that the petals become effective. His ideas and conceptions must be guarded; each single idea should acquire significance for him; he should see in it a definite message instructing him concerning the things of the outer world, and he should derive no satisfaction from ideas devoid of such significance. He must govern his mental life so that it becomes a true mirror of the outer world, and direct his effort to the exclusion of incorrect ideas from his soul.

137

The second of these functions is concerned with the control of resolutions. The student must not resolve upon even the most trifling act without well-founded and thorough consideration. Thoughtless and meaningless actions should be foreign to his nature. He should have well-considered grounds for everything he does, and abstain from everything to which no significant motive urges him.

The third function concerns speech. The student should utter no word that is devoid of sense and meaning; all talking for the sake of talking draws him away from his path. He must avoid the usual kind of conversation, with its promiscuous discussion of indiscriminately varied topics. This does not imply his preclusion from intercourse with his fellows. It is precisely in such intercourse that his conversation should develop to significance. He is ready to converse with everyone, but he does so thoughtfully and with thorough deliberation. He never speaks without grounds for what he says. He seeks to use neither too many nor too few words.

The fourth is the regulation of outward action. The student tries to adjust his actions in such a

138

way that they harmonize with the actions of his fellow-men and with the events in his environment. He refrains from actions which are disturbing to others and in conflict with his surroundings. He seeks to adjust his actions so that they combine harmoniously with his surroundings and with his position in life. When an external motive causes him to act he considers how he can best respond. When the impulse proceeds from himself he weighs with minute care the effects of his activity.

The fifth function includes the management of the whole of life. The student endeavors to live in conformity with both nature and spirit. Never overhasty, he is also never indolent. Excessive activity and laziness are equally alien to him. He looks upon life as a means for work and disposes it accordingly. He regulates his habits and the care of his health in such a way that a harmonious whole is the outcome.

The sixth is concerned with human endeavor. The student tests his capacities and proficiency, and conducts himself in the light of such self-knowledge. He attempts nothing beyond his powers, yet seeks to omit nothing within their scope.

On the other hand, he sets himself aims that have to do with the ideals and the great duties of a human being. He does not mechanically regard himself as a wheel in the vast machinery of mankind but seeks to comprehend the tasks of his life, and to look out beyond the limit of the daily and trivial. He endeavors to fulfill his obligations ever better and more perfectly.

The seventh deals with the effort to learn as much from life as possible. Nothing passes before the student without giving him occasion to accumulate experience which is of value to him for life. If he has performed anything wrongly or imperfectly, he lets this be an incentive for meeting the same contingency later on rightly and perfectly. When others act he observes them with the same end in view. He tries to gather a rich store of experience, ever returning to it for counsel; nor indeed will he ever do anything without looking back on experiences from which he can derive help in his decisions and affairs.

Finally, the eighth is as follows: The student must, from time to time, glance introspectively into himself, sink back into himself, take counsel with himself, form and test the fundamental prin-

ciples of his life, run over in his thoughts the sum total of his knowledge, weigh his duties, and reflect upon the content and aim of life. All these things have been mentioned in the preceding chapters; here they are merely recapitulated in connection with the development of the sixteen-petalled lotus. By means of these exercises the latter will become ever more and more perfect, for it is upon such exercises that the development of clairvoyance depends. The better the student's thoughts and speech harmonize with the processes in the outer world, the more quickly will he develop this faculty. Whoever thinks and speaks what is contrary to truth destroys something in the germ of his sixteen-petalled lotus. Truthfulness, uprightness, and honesty are in this connection creative forces, while mendacity, deceitfulness, and dishonesty are destructive forces. The student must realize, however, that actual deeds are needed, and not merely good intentions. If I think or say anything that does not conform with reality, I kill something in my spiritual organs, even though I believe my intentions to be ever so good. It is here as with the child which needs must burn itself when it touches

141

fire, even though it did so out of ignorance. The regulation of the above activities of the soul in the manner described causes the sixteen-petalled lotus to shine in glorious hues, and imparts to it a definite movement. Yet it must be noted that the faculty of clairvoyance cannot make its appearance before a definite degree of development of the soul has been reached. It cannot appear as long as it is irksome for the student to regulate his life in this manner. He is still unfit as long as the activities described above are a matter of special pre-occupation for him. The first traces of clairvoyance only appear when he has reached the point of being able to live in the specified way, as a person habitually lives. These things must then no longer be laborious, but must have become a matter of course. There must be no need for him to be continually watching himself and urging himself on to live in this way. It must all have become a matter of habit.

Now this lotus flower may be made to develop in another way by following certain other instructions. But all such methods are rejected by true spiritual science, for they lead to the destruction of physical health and to moral ruin.

They are easier to follow than those here described. The latter, though protracted and difficult, lead to the true goal and cannot but strengthen morally.

The distorted development of a lotus flower results not only in illusions and fantastic conceptions, should a certain degree of clairvoyance be acquired, but also in errors and instability in ordinary life. Such a development may be the cause of timidity, envy, vanity, haughtiness, wilfulness and so on in a person who hitherto was free from these defects. It has already been explained that eight of the sixteen petals of this lotus flower were developed in a remote past, and that these will re-appear of themselves in the course of esoteric development. All the effort and attention of the student must be devoted to the remaining eight. Faulty training may easily result in the re-appearance of the earlier petals alone, while the new petals remain stunted. This will ensue especially if too little logical, rational thinking is employed in the training. It is of supreme importance that the student should be a rational and clear-thinking person, and of further importance that he should practice the greatest

143

clarity of speech. People who begin to have some presentiment of supersensible things are apt to wax talkative on this subject, thereby retarding their normal development. The less one talks about these matters the better. Only someone who has achieved a certain degree of clarity should speak about them. At the beginning of their instruction, students are as a rule astonished at the teacher's lack of curiosity concerning their own experiences. It would be much better for them to remain entirely silent on this subject, and to content themselves with mentioning only whether they have been successful or unsuccessful in performing the exercises and observing the instructions given them. For the teacher has quite other means of estimating their progress than the students' own statements. The eight petals now under consideration always become a little hardened through such statements, whereas they should be kept soft and supple. The following example taken, for the sake of clarity, not from the supersensible world but from ordinary life, will illustrate this point. Suppose I hear a piece of news and thereupon immediately form an opinion. Shortly afterwards I receive some further news which does not tally with the previous information. I am thereby obliged to reverse my previous judgment. The result is an unfavorable influence upon my sixteen-petalled lotus. Quite the contrary would have been the case had I, in the first place, suspended judgment, and remained silent both inwardly in thought and outwardly in word concerning the whole affair, until I had acquired reliable grounds for forming my judgment. Caution in the formation and pronouncement of judgments becomes, by degrees, the special characteristic of the student. On the other hand his receptivity for impressions and experiences increases; he lets them pass over him silently, so as to collect and have the largest possible number of facts at his disposal when the time comes to form his opinions. Bluish-red and reddish-pink shades color the lotus flower as the result of such circumspection, whereas in the opposite case dark red and orange shades appear. (Students will recognize in the conditions attached to the development of the sixteen-petalled lotus the instructions given by the Buddha to his disciples for the *Path*. Yet there is no question here of teaching Buddhism, but of describing conditions governing development which are the natural outcome of spiritual science. The fact that these conditions correspond with certain teachings of the Buddha is no reason for not finding them true in themselves.)

The twelve-petalled lotus situated in the region of the heart is developed in a similar way. Half its petals, too, were already existent and in active use in a remote stage of human evolution. Hence these six petals need not now be especially developed in esoteric training; they appear of themselves and begin to revolve when the student sets to work on the other six. Here again he learns to promote this development by consciously controlling and directing certain inner activities in a special way.

It must be clearly understood that the perceptions of each single organ of soul or spirit bear a different character. The twelve and sixteen-petalled lotus flowers transmit quite different perceptions. The latter perceives forms. The thoughts and mentality of other beings and the laws governing natural phenomena become manifest, through the sixteen-petalled lotus, as figures, not rigid motionless figures but mobile forms

146

filled with life. The clairvoyant in whom this sense is developed can describe, for every mode of thought and for every law of nature, a form which expresses them. A revengeful thought, for example, assumes an arrow-like, pronged form, while a kindly thought is often formed like an opening flower, and so on. Clear-cut, significant thoughts are regular and symmetrical in form, while confused thoughts have wavy outlines. Quite different perceptions are received through the twelve-petalled lotus. These perceptions may, in a sense, be likened to warmth and cold, as applied to the soul. A clairvoyant equipped with this faculty feels this warmth and cold streaming out from the forms discerned by the sixteen-petalled lotus. Had he developed the sixteen and not the twelve-petalled lotus he would only perceive, in the kindly thought, for instance, the figure described above, while a clairvoyant in whom both senses were developed would also notice what can only be described as soul-warmth, flowing from the thought. It should be noted in passing that esoteric training never develops one organ without the other, so that the above-mentioned example may be regarded as a hypothetical case in behalf of clarity. The twelve-petalled lotus, when developed, reveals to the clairvoyant a deep understanding of the processes of nature. Rays of soul-warmth issue from every manifestation of growth and development, while everything in the process of decay, destruction, ruin, gives an impression of cold.

The development of this sense may be furthered in the following manner. *To begin with, the student endeavors to regulate his sequence of thought (control of thought)*. Just as the sixteen-petalled lotus is developed by cultivating thoughts that conform with truth and are significant, so, too, the twelve-petalled lotus is developed by inwardly controlling the trains of thought. Thoughts that dart to and fro like will-o'-the-wisps and follow each other in no logical or rational sequence, but merely by pure chance, destroy its form. The closer thought is made to follow upon thought, and the more strictly everything of illogical nature is avoided, the more suitable will be the form this sense organ develops. If the student hears illogical thoughts he immediately lets the right thoughts pass through his mind. He should not, however, withdraw

148

in a loveless way from what is perhaps an illogical environment in order to further his own development. Neither should he feel himself impelled to correct all the illogical thoughts expressed around him. He should rather silently co-ordinate the thoughts as they pour in upon him, and make them conform to logic and sense, and at the same time endeavor in every case to retain this same method in his own thinking.

An equal consistency in his actions forms the second requirement (control of actions). All inconstancy, all disharmony of action, is baneful for the lotus flower here in question. When the student performs some action he must see to it that his succeeding action follows in logical sequence, for if he acts from day to day with variable intent he will never develop the faculty here considered.

The third requirement is the cultivation of endurance (perseverance). The student is impervious to all influences which would divert him from the goal he has set himself, as long as he can regard it as the right goal. For him, obstacles contain a challenge that impels him to surmount them, but never a reason for giving up.

The fourth requirement is forbearance (tolerance) toward persons, creatures, and also circumstances. The student suppresses all superfluous criticism of everything that is imperfect, evil and bad, and seeks rather to understand everything that comes under his notice. Even as the sun does not withdraw its light from the bad and the evil, so he, too, does not refuse them an intelligent sympathy. Should some trouble befall him he does not proceed to condemn and criticize, but accepts the inevitable, and endeavors to the best of his ability to give the matter a turn for the best. He does not consider the opinions of others merely from his own standpoint, but seeks to put himself into the other's position.

The fifth requirement is impartiality toward everything that life brings. In this connection we speak of faith and trust. The student meets every human being and every creature with this trust, and lets it inspire his every action. Upon hearing some information, he never says to himself: "I don't believe it; it contradicts my present opinions." He is far rather ready to test and rectify his views and opinions. He ever remains receptive for everything that confronts him, and he trusts in the efficacy of his undertakings. Timidity and scepticism are banished from his being. He harbors a faith in the power of his intentions. A hundred failures cannot rob him of this faith. This is the *"faith which can move mountains."*

The sixth requirement is the cultivation of a certain inner balance (equanimity). The student endeavors to retain his composure in the face of joy and sorrow, and eradicates the tendency to fluctuate between the seventh heaven of joy and the depths of despair. Misfortune and danger, fortune and advancement alike find him ready armed.

The reader will recognize in the qualities here described the *six attributes* which the candidate for initiation strives to acquire. The intention has been to show their connection with the spiritual organ known as the twelve-petalled lotus flower. As before, special instructions can be given to bring this lotus flower to fruition, but here again the perfect symmetry of its form depends on the development of the qualities mentioned, the neglect of which results in this organ being formed into a caricature of its proper shape. In this case, should a certain clairvoyance be attained, the qualities in question may take an evil instead of a good direction. A person may become intolerant, timid, or contentious toward his environment; may, for instance, acquire some feeling for the sentiments of others, and for this reason shun them or hate them. This may even reach the point where, by reason of the inner coldness that overwhelms him when he hears repugnant opinions, he is unable to listen, or he may behave in an objectionable manner.

The development of this organ may be accelerated if, in addition to all that has been stated, certain other injunctions are observed which can only be imparted to the student by word of mouth. Yet the instructions given above do actually lead to genuine esoteric training, and moreover, the regulation of life in the way described can be advantageous to all who cannot or will not undergo esoteric training. For it does not fail to produce an effect upon the organism of the soul, even though slowly. As regards the esoteric student, the observance of these principles is indispensable. Should he attempt esoteric training without conforming to them, this could only result in his entering the higher worlds with inadequate organs, and instead of perceiving the truth he would be subject to deceptions and illusions. He would attain a certain clairvoyance, but for the most part, be the victim of greater blindness than before. Formerly he at least stood firmly within the physical world; now he looks beyond this physical world and grows confused about it before acquiring a firm footing in a higher world. All power of distinguishing truth from error would then perhaps fail him, and he would entirely lose his way in life. It is just for this reason that patience is so necessary in these matters. It must ever be borne in mind that the instructions given in esoteric training may go no further than is compatible with the willing readiness shown to develop the lotus flowers to their regular shape. Should these flowers be brought to fruition before they have quietly attained their correct form, mere caricatures would be the result. Their maturity can be brought about by the special instructions given in esoteric training, but their form is dependent on the method of life described above.

An inner training of a particularly intimate character is necessary for the development of the ten-petalled lotus flower, for it is now a question of learning consciously to control and dominate the sense-impressions themselves. This is of particular importance in the initial stages of clairvoyance, for it is only by this means that a source of countless illusions and fancies is avoided. People as a rule do not realize by what factors their sudden ideas and memories are dominated, and how they are produced. Consider the following case. Someone is travelling by railway; his mind is busy with one thought; suddenly his thought diverges; he recollects an experience that befell him years ago and interweaves it with his present thought. He did not notice that in looking through the window he had caught sight of a person who resembled another intimately connected with the recollected experience. He remains conscious, not of what he saw, but of the effect it produced, and thus believes that it all came to him of its own accord. How much in life occurs in such a way! How great is the part played in our life by things we hear and learn, without our consciously realizing the connection! Someone, for instance, cannot bear a certain color, but does not realize that this is due

154

to the fact that the schoolteacher who used to worry him many years ago wore a coat of that color. Innumerable illusions are based upon such associations. Many things leave their mark upon the soul while remaining outside the pale of consciousness. The following may occur. Someone reads in the paper about the death of a well-known person, and forthwith claims to have had a presentiment of it yesterday, although he had neither heard nor seen anything that might have given rise to such a thought. And indeed it is quite true that the thought occurred to him yesterday, as though of its own accord, that this particular person would die; only one thing escaped his attention: two or three hours before this thought occurred to him yesterday, he went to visit an acquaintance; a newspaper lay on the table; he did not actually read it, but his eyes unconsciously fell on the announcement of the dangerous illness of the person in question. He remained unconscious of the impression he had received, and yet this impression resulted in his presentiment.

Reflection upon these matters will show how great is the source of illusion and fantasy contained in such associations. It is just this source which must be dammed up by all who seek to develop their ten-petalled lotus flower. Deeply hidden characteristics in other souls can be perceived by this organ, but their truth depends on the attainment of immunity from the above-mentioned illusions. For this purpose it is necessary that the student should control and dominate everything that seeks to influence him from outside. He should reach the point of really receiving no impressions beyond those he wishes to receive. This can only be achieved by the development of a powerful inner life; by an effort of the will he only allows such things to impress him to which his attention is directed, and he actually evades all impressions to which he does not voluntarily respond. If he sees something it is because he wills to see it, and if he does not voluntarily take notice of something it is actually non-existent for him. The greater the energy and inner activity devoted to this work, the more extensively will this faculty be attained. The student must avoid all vacuous gazing and mechanical listening. For him only those things exist to which he turns his eye or his ear. He must practice the power of hearing nothing, even in the greatest disturbance, if he does not will to hear; and he must make his eyes unimpressionable to things of which he does not particularly take notice. He must be shielded as by an inner armor against all unconscious impressions. In this connection the student must devote special care to his thought-life. He singles out a particular thought and endeavors to link with it only such other thoughts as he can himself consciously and voluntarily produce. He rejects all casual ideas and does not connect this thought with another until he has investigated the origin of the latter. He goes still further. If, for instance, he feels a particular antipathy for something, he will combat it and endeavor to establish a conscious relation between himself and the thing in question. In this way the unconscious elements that intrude into his soul will become fewer and fewer. Only by such severe self-discipline can the ten-petalled lotus flower attain its proper form. The student's inner life must become a life of attention, and he must learn really to hold at a distance everything to which he should not or does not wish to direct his attention.

If this strict self-discipline be accompanied by meditation as prescribed in esoteric training, the lotus flower in the region of the pit of the stomach comes to maturity in the right way, and light and color of a spiritual kind are now added to the form and warmth perceptible to the organs described above. The talents and faculties of other beings are thereby revealed, also the forces and the hidden attributes of nature. The colored aura of living creatures then becomes visible; all that is around us manifests its spiritual attributes. It must be understood that the very greatest care is necessary at this stage of development, for the play of unconscious memories is here exceedingly active. If this were not the case, many people would possess this inner sense, for it comes almost immediately into evidence when the impressions delivered by the outer senses are held so completely under control that they become dependent on nothing save attention or inattention. This inner sense remains ineffective as long as the powerful outer senses smother and benumb it.

Still greater difficulty attends the development of the six-petalled lotus flower situated in the center of the body, for it can only be achieved as

158

the result of complete mastery and control of the whole personality through consciousness of self, so that body, soul, and spirit form one harmonious whole. The functions of the body, the inclinations and passions of the soul, the thoughts and ideas of the spirit must be tuned to perfect unison. The body must be so ennobled and purified that its organs incite to nothing that is not in the service of the soul and spirit. The soul must not be impelled through the body to lusts and passions which are antagonistic to pure and noble thought. Yet the spirit must not stand like a slave-driver over the soul, dominating it with laws and commandments; the soul must rather learn to obey these laws and duties out of its own free inclination. The student must not feel duty to be an oppressive power to which he unwillingly submits, but rather something which he performs out of love. His task is to develop a free soul that maintains equilibrium between body and spirit, and he must perfect himself in this way to the extent of being free to abandon himself to the functions of the senses, for these should be so purified that they lose the power to drag him down to their level. He must no longer require to curb his passions, in as much as they of their own accord follow the good. So long as self-chastisement is necessary, no one can pass a certain stage of esoteric development; for a virtue practiced under constraint is futile. If there is any lust remaining, it interferes with esoteric development, however great the effort made not to humor it. Nor does it matter whether this desire proceeds from the soul or the body. For example, if a certain stimulant be avoided for the purpose of self-purification, this deprivation will only prove helpful if the body suffers no harm from it. Should the contrary be the case, this proves that the body craves the stimulant, and that abstinence from it is of no value. In this case it may actually be a question of renouncing the ideal to be attained, until more favorable physical conditions, perhaps in another life, shall be forthcoming. A wise renunciation may be a far greater achievement than the struggle for something which, under given conditions, remains unattainable. Indeed, a renunciation of this kind contributes more toward development than the opposite course.

The six-petalled lotus flower, when developed, permits of intercourse with beings of higher worlds, though only when their existence is manifested in the astral or soul-world. The development of this lotus flower, however, is not advisable unless the student has made great progress on that path of esoteric development which enables him to raise his spirit into a still higher world. This entry into the spiritual world proper must always run parallel with the development of the lotus flowers, otherwise the student will fall into error and confusion. He would undoubtedly be able to see, but he would remain incapable of forming a correct estimate of what he saw. Now, the development of the six-petalled lotus flower itself provides a certain security against confusion and instability, for no one can be easily confused who has attained perfect equilibrium between sense (or body), passion (or soul), and idea (or spirit). And yet, something more than this security is required when, through the development of the six-petalled lotus flower, living beings of independent existence are revealed to his spirit, beings belonging to a world so completely different from the world known to his physical senses. The development of the lotus flowers alone does not assure sufficient security in these higher worlds; still higher organs are necessary. The latter will now be described before the remaining lotus flowers and the further organization of the soul-body are discussed. (This expression—soul-body—although obviously contradictory when taken literally, is used because to clairvoyant perception the impression received spiritually corresponds to the impression received physically when the physical body is perceived.)

The development of the soul-body in the manner described above permits of perception in a supersensible world, but anyone wishing to find his way in this world must not remain stationary at this stage of development. The mere mobility of the lotus flowers is not sufficient. The student must acquire the power of regulating and controlling the movement of his spiritual organs independently and with complete consciousness; otherwise he would become a plaything for external forces and powers. To avoid this he must acquire the faculty of hearing what is called the *inner word,* and this involves the development not only of the soul-body but also of the etheric

162

body. The latter is that tenuous body revealed to the clairvoyant as a kind of double of the physical body, and forms to a certain extent an intermediate step between the soul nature and the physical body. (See the description in the author's book *Theosophy*.) It is possible for one equipped with clairvoyant powers consciously to suggest away the physical body of a person. This corresponds on a higher plane to an exercise in attentiveness on a lower plane. Just as a person can divert his attention from something in front of him so that it becomes non-existent for him, the clairvoyant can extinguish a physical body from his field of observation so that it becomes physically transparent to him. If he exerts this faculty in the case of some person standing before him, there remains visible to his clairvoyant sight only the etheric body, besides the soul-body which is larger than the other two—etheric and physical bodies—and interpenetrates them both. The etheric body has approximately the size and form of the physical body, so that it practically fills the same space. It is an extremely delicate and finely organized structure. (I beg the physicist not to be disturbed at the expression "etheric

163

body". The word ether here is merely used to suggest the fineness of the body in question, and need not in any way be connected with the hypothetical ether of physics.)

Its ground-color is different from any of the seven colors contained in the rainbow. Anyone capable of observing it will find a color which is actually non-existent for sense perception but to which the color of young peach-blossom may be comparable. If desired, the etheric body can be examined alone; for this purpose the soul-body must be extinguished by an effort of attentiveness in the manner described above. Otherwise the etheric body will present an ever changing picture owing to its interpenetration by the soul-body.

Now, the particles of the etheric body are in continual motion. Countless currents stream through it in every direction. By these currents, life itself is maintained and regulated. Every body that has life, including animals and plants, possesses an etheric body. Even in minerals traces of it can be observed. These currents and movements are, to begin with, independent of human will and consciousness, just as the action of the

164

heart or stomach is beyond our jurisdiction, and this independence remains unaltered so long as we do not take our development in hand in the sense of acquiring supersensible faculties. For, at a certain stage, development consists precisely in adding to the unconscious currents and movements of the etheric body others that are consciously produced and controlled.

When esoteric development has progressed so far that the lotus flowers begin to stir, much has already been achieved by the student which can result in the formation of certain quite definite currents and movements in his etheric body. The object of this development is the formation of a kind of center in the region of the physical heart, from which radiate currents and movements in the greatest possible variety of colors and forms. The center is in reality not a mere point, but a most complicated structure, a most wonderful organ. It glows and shimmers with every shade of color and displays forms of great symmetry, capable of rapid transformation. Other forms and streams of color radiate from this organ to the other parts of the body, and beyond it to the astral body, completely permeating and illumi-

165

nating it. The most important of these currents flow to the lotus flowers. They permeate each petal and regulate its revolutions; then streaming out at the points of the petals, they lose themselves in outer space. The higher the development of a person, the greater the circumference to which these rays extend.

The twelve-petalled lotus flower has a particularly close connection with this central organ. The currents flow directly into it and through it, proceeding on the one side to the sixteen and the two-petalled lotus flowers, and on the other, the lower side, to the flowers of eight, six and four petals. It is for this reason that the very greatest care must be devoted to the development of the twelve-petalled lotus, for an imperfection in the latter would result in the irregular formation of the whole structure. The above will give an idea of the delicate and intimate nature of esoteric training, and of the accuracy needed if the development is to be regular and correct. It will also be evident beyond doubt that directions for the development of supersensible faculties can only be the concern of those who have themselves experienced everything which they propose to awaken in others, and who are unquestionably in a position to know whether the directions they give lead to the exact results desired. If the student follows the directions that have been given him, he introduces into his etheric body currents and movements which are in harmony with the laws and the evolution of the world to which he belongs. Consequently these instructions are reflections of the great laws of cosmic evolution. They consist of the above-mentioned and similar exercises in meditation and concentration which, if correctly practiced, produce the results described. The student must at certain times let these instructions permeate his soul with their content, so that he is inwardly entirely filled with it. A simple start is made with a view to the deepening of the logical activity of the mind and the producing of an inward intensification of thought. Thought is thereby made free and independent of all sense impressions and experiences; it is concentrated in one point which is held entirely under control. Thus a preliminary center is formed for the currents of the etheric body. This center is not yet in the region of the heart but in the head, and it appears to the clair-

167

voyant as the point of departure for movements and currents. No esoteric training can be successful which does not first create this center. If the latter were first formed in the region of the heart the aspiring clairvoyant would doubtless obtain glimpses of the higher worlds, but would lack all true insight into the connection between these higher worlds and the world of our senses. This, however, is an unconditional necessity for man at the present stage of evolution. The clairvoyant must not become a visionary; he must retain a firm footing upon the earth.

The center in the head, once duly fixed, is then moved lower down, to the region of the larynx. This is effected by further exercises in concentration. Then the currents of the etheric body radiate from this point and illumine the astral space surrounding the individual.

Continued practice enables the student to determine for himself the position of his etheric body. Hitherto this position depended upon external forces proceeding from the physical body. Through further development the student is able to turn his etheric body to all sides. This faculty is effected by currents moving approximately along both hands and centered in the two-petalled lotus in the region of the eyes. All this is made possible through the radiations from the larynx assuming round forms, of which a number flow to the two-petalled lotus and thence form undulating currents along the hands. As a further development, these currents branch out and ramify in the most delicate manner and become, as it were, a kind of web which then encompasses the entire etheric body as though with a network. Whereas hitherto the etheric body was not closed to the outer world, so that the life currents from the universal ocean of life flowed freely in and out, these currents now have to pass through this membrane. Thus the individual becomes sensitive to these external streams; they become perceptible to him.

And now the time has come to give the complete system of currents and movements its center situated in the region of the heart. This again is effected by persevering with the exercises in concentration and mediation; and at this point also the stage is reached when the student becomes gifted with the inner word. All things now acquire a new significance for him. They become as it were spiritually audible in their innermost self, and speak to him of their essential being. The currents described above place him in touch with the inner being of the world to which he belongs. He begins to mingle his life with the life of his environment and can let it reverberate in the movements of his lotus flowers.

At this point the spiritual world is entered. If the student has advanced so far, he acquires a new understanding for all that the great teachers of humanity have uttered. The sayings of the Buddha and the Gospels, for instance, produce a new effect on him. They pervade him with a rapture of which he had not dreamed before. For the tone of their words follows the movements and rhythms which he has himself formed within himself. He can now have positive knowledge that a Buddha or the Evangelists did not utter their own revelations but those which flowed into them from the inmost being of all things. A fact must here be pointed out which can only be understood in the light of what has been said above. The many repetitions in the sayings of the Buddha are not comprehensible to people of our present evolutionary stage. For the esoteric stu-

170

dent, however, they become a force on which he gladly lets his inner senses rest, for they correspond with certain movements in the etheric body. Devotional surrender to them, with perfect inner peace, creates an inner harmony with these movements; and because the latter are an image of certain cosmic rhythms which also at certain points repeat themselves and revert to former modes, the student listening to the wisdom of the Buddha unites his life with that of the cosmic mysteries.

In esoteric training there is question of *four attributes* which must be acquired on the so-called preparatory path for the attainment of higher knowledge. *The first* is the faculty of discriminating in thoughts between truth and appearance or mere opinion. *The second* attribute is the correct estimation of what is inwardly true and real, as against what is merely apparent. *The third* rests in the practice of the six qualities already mentioned in the preceding pages: thought-control, control of actions, perseverance, tolerance, faith, and equanimity. *The fourth* attribute is the love of inner freedom.

A mere intellectual understanding of what is

171

included in these attributes is of no value. They must be so incorporated into the soul that they form the basis of inner habits. Consider, for instance, the first of these attributes: the discrimination between truth and appearance. The student must so train himself that, as a matter of course, he distinguishes in everything that confronts him between the non-essential elements and those that are significant and essential. He will only succeed in this if, in his observation of the outer world, he quietly and patiently ever and again repeats the attempt. And at the end he will naturally single out the essential and the true at a glance, whereas formerly the non-essential, the transient, too, could content him. "All that is transient is but a seeming"* is a truth which becomes an unquestionable conviction of the soul. The same applies to the remaining three of the four attributes mentioned.

Now these four inner habits do actually produce a transformation of the delicate human etheric body. By the first, discrimination between truth and appearance, the center in the head al-

* *"Alles Vergängliche ist nur ein Gleichnis,"* Goethe, *Faust II.*

ready described is formed and the center in the region of the larynx prepared. The actual development of these centers is of course dependent on the exercises in concentration described above; the latter make for development and the four attributes bring to fruition. Once the center in the larynx has been prepared, the free control of the etheric body and its enclosure within a network covering, as explained above, results from the correct estimation of what is true as against what is apparent and non-essential. If the student acquires this faculty of estimation, the facts of the higher worlds will gradually become perceptible to him. But he must not think that he has to perform only such actions which appear significant when judged by the standard of a mere intellectual estimate. The most trifling action, every little thing accomplished, has something of importance in the great cosmic household, and it is merely a question of being aware of this importance. A correct estimation of the affairs of daily life is required, not an underestimation of them. The six virtues of which the third attribute consists have already been dealt with; they are connected with the development of the twelve-

173

petalled lotus in the region of the heart, and, as already indicated, it is to this center that the life-currents of the etheric body must be directed. The fourth attribute, the longing for liberation, serves to bring to fruition the etheric organ in the heart region. Once this attribute becomes an inner habit, the individual frees himself from everything which depends only upon the faculties of his own personal nature. He ceases to view things from his own separate standpoint, and the boundaries of his own narrow self fettering him to this point of view disappear. The secrets of the spiritual world gain access to his inner self. This is liberation. For those fetters constrain the individual to regard things and beings in a manner corresponding to his own personal traits. It is from this personal manner of regarding things that the student must become liberated and free.

It will be clear from the above that the instructions given in esoteric training exert a determining influence reaching the innermost depths of human nature. Such are the instructions regarding the four qualities mentioned above. They can be found in one form or another in all the great cosmogonies that take account of the spiritual world. The founders of the great cosmogonies did not give mankind these teachings from some vague feeling. They gave them for the good reason that they were great initiates. Out of their knowledge did they shape their moral teachings. They knew how these would act upon the finer nature of man, and desired that their followers should gradually achieve the development of this finer nature. To live in the sense of these great cosmogonies means to work for the attainment of personal spiritual perfection. Only by so doing can man become a servant of the world and of humanity. Self-perfection is by no means self-seeking, for the imperfect man is an imperfect servant of the world and of humanity. The more perfect a man is, the better does he serve the world. "If the rose adorns itself, it adorns the garden."

The founders of the great cosmogonies are therefore the great initiates. Their teaching flows into the soul of men, and thus, with humanity, the whole world moves forward. Quite consciously did they work to further this evolutionary process of humanity. Their teachings can only be understood if it be remembered that they are the product of knowledge of the innermost depths of human nature. The great initiates knew, and it is out of their knowledge that they shaped the ideals of humanity. And man approaches these great leaders when he uplifts himself, in his own development, to their heights.

A completely new life opens out before the student when the development of his etheric body begins in the way described above, and at the proper time, in the course of his training, he must receive that enlightenment which enables him to adapt himself to this new existence. The sixteen-petalled lotus, for instance, enables him to perceive spiritual figures of a higher world. He must learn now how different these figures can be when caused by different objects or beings. In the first place, he must notice that his own thoughts and feelings exert a powerful influence on certain of these figures, on others little or no influence. One kind of figure alters immediately if the observer, upon seeing it, says to himself: "that is beautiful," and then in the course of his observation changes this thought to: "that is useful." It is characteristic of the forms proceeding from minerals or from artificial objects that they change

176

under the influence of every thought and every feeling directed upon them by the observer. This applies in a lesser degree to the forms belonging to plants, and still less to those corresponding to animals. These figures, too, are full of life and motion, but this motion is only partially due to the influence of human thoughts and feelings; in other respects it is produced by causes which are beyond human influence. Now, there appears within this whole world a species of form which remains almost entirely unaffected by human influence. The student can convince himself that these forms proceed neither from minerals nor from artificial objects, nor, again, from plants or animals. To gain complete understanding, he must study those forms which he can realize to have proceeded from the feelings, instincts, and passions of human beings. Yet he can find that these forms too are influenced by his own thoughts and feelings, if only to a relatively small extent. But there always remains a residuum of forms in this world upon which such influences are negligible. Indeed, at the outset of his career the student can perceive little beyond this residuum. He can only discover its nature by observing himself. He then learns what forms he himself produces, for his will, his wishes, and so on, are expressed in these forms. An instinct that dwells in him, a desire that fills him, an intention that he harbors, and so forth, are all manifested in these forms: his whole character displays itself in this world of forms. Thus by his conscious thoughts and feelings a person can exercise an influence on all forms which do not proceed from himself; but over those which he brings about in the higher world through his own being he possesses no power, once he has created them. Now, it follows from what has been said that on this higher plane man's inner life of instincts, desires, ideas displays itself outwardly in definite forms, just like all other beings and objects. To higher knowledge, the inner world appears as part of the outer world. In a higher world man's inner being confronts him as a reflected image, just as though in the physical world he were surrounded by mirrors and could observe his physical body in that way.

At this stage of development the student has reached the point where he can free himself from the illusion resulting from the limitation of his

178

personal self. He can now observe that inner self as outer world, just as he hitherto regarded as outer world everything that affected his senses. Thus he learns by gradual experience to deal with himself as hitherto he dealt with the beings around him.

Were the student to obtain an insight into these spiritual worlds without sufficient preparation regarding their nature, he would find himself confronted by the picture of his own soul as though by an enigma. There his own desires and passions confront him in animal or, more rarely, in human forms. It is true that the animal forms of this world are never quite similar to those of the physical world, yet they possess a remote resemblance: inexpert observers often take them to be identical. Now, upon entering this world, an entirely new method of judgment must be acquired; for apart from the fact that things actually pertaining to inner nature appear as outer world, they also bear the character of mirrored reflections of what they really are. When, for instance, a number is perceived, it must be read in reverse, as a picture in a mirror; 265 would mean here in reality 562. A sphere is perceived as though from its center. This inner perception must then be translated in the right way. The qualities of the soul appear likewise as in a mirror. A wish directed toward an outer object appears as a form moving toward the person wishing. Passions residing in the lower part of human nature can assume animal forms or similar shapes that hurl themselves against the individual. In reality, these passions are headed outward; they seek satisfaction in the outer world, but this striving outward appears in the mirrored reflection as an attack on the individual from whom they proceed.

If the student, before attaining insight into higher worlds, has learned by quiet and sincere self-observation to realize the qualities and defects of his own character, he will then, at the moment when his own inner self confronts him as a mirrored image, find strength and courage to conduct himself in the right way. People who have failed to test themselves in this way, and are insufficiently acquainted with their own inner self, will not recognize themselves in their own mirrored image and will mistake it for an alien reality. Or they may become alarmed at the vision and, because they cannot endure the sight, deceive themselves into believing the whole thing is nothing but an illusion which cannot lead them anywhere. In either case the person in question, through prematurely attaining a certain stage of inner development, would fatally obstruct his own progress.

It is absolutely necessary that the student should experience this spiritual aspect of his own inner self before progressing to higher spheres; for his own self constitutes that psycho-spiritual element of which he is the best judge. If he has thoroughly realized the nature of his own personality in the physical world, and if the image of his personality first appears to him in a higher world, he is then able to compare the one with the other. He can refer the higher to something already known to him, so that his point of departure is on firm ground. Whereas, no matter how many other spiritual beings appeared to him, he would find himself unable to discover their nature and qualities, and would soon feel the ground giving way beneath him. Thus it cannot be too often repeated that the only safe entrance into the higher worlds is at the end of a path leading through a genuine knowledge and estimate of one's own nature.

Pictures, then, of a spiritual kind are first encountered by the student on his progress into higher worlds; and the reality to which these pictures correspond is actually within himself. He should be far enough advanced to refrain from desiring reality of a more robust kind at this initial stage, and to regard these pictures as timely. He will soon meet something quite new within this world of pictures. His lower self is before him as a mirrored image; but from within this image there appears the true reality of his higher self. Out of the picture of his lower personality the form of the spiritual ego becomes visible. Then threads are spun from the latter to other and higher spiritual realities.

This is the moment when the two-petalled lotus in the region of the eyes is required. If it now begins to stir, the student finds it possible to bring his higher ego in contact with higher spiritual beings. The currents from this lotus flower flow toward the higher realities in such a way that the movements in question are fully apparent to the individual. Just as the light renders the physical objects visible, so, too, these currents disclose spiritual beings of higher worlds.

Through inward application to the fundamental truths derived from spiritual science the student learns to set in motion and then to direct the currents proceeding from the lotus flower between the eyes.

It is at this stage of development especially that the value of sound judgment and a training in clear and logical thought come to the fore. The higher self, which hitherto slumbered unconsciously in an embryonic state, is now born into conscious existence. This is not a figurative but a positive birth in the spiritual world, and the being now born, the higher self, must enter that world with all the necessary organs and aptitudes if it is to be capable of life. Just as nature must provide for a child being born into the world with suitable eyes and ears, so too, the laws of self-development must provide for the necessary capacities with which the higher self can enter existence. These laws governing the development of the higher spiritual organs are none other than the laws of sound reason and morality of the physical world. The spiritual self matures in the

183

physical self as a child in the mother's womb. The child's health depends upon the normal functioning of natural laws in the maternal womb. The constitution of the spiritual self is similarly conditioned by the laws of common intelligence and reason that govern physical life. No one can give birth to a soundly constituted higher self whose life in thought and feeling, in the physical world, is not sound and healthy. Natural, rational life is the basis of all genuine spiritual development. Just as the child when still in the maternal womb lives in accordance with the natural forces to which it has access, after its birth, through its organs of sense, so, too, the human higher self lives in accordance with the laws of the spiritual world, even during physical existence. And even as the child, out of a dim life instinct, acquires the requisite forces, so, too, can man acquire the powers of the spiritual world before his higher self is born. Indeed, he must do this if the latter is to enter the world as a fully developed being. It would be quite wrong for anyone to say: "I cannot accept the teachings of spiritual science until I myself become a seer," for without inward application

184

to the results of spiritual research there is no chance whatever of attaining genuine higher knowledge. It would be as though a child, during gestation, were to refuse the forces coming to it through its mother, and proposed to wait until it could procure them for itself. Just as the embryonic child in its incipient feeling for life learns to appreciate what is offered to it, so can the non-seer appreciate the truth of the teachings of spiritual science. An insight into these teachings based on a deeply rooted feeling for truth, and a clear, sound, all-round critical and reasoning faculty are possible even before spiritual things are actually perceived. The esoteric knowledge must first be studied, so that this study becomes a preparation for clairvoyance. A person attaining clairvoyance without such preparation would resemble a child born with eyes and ears but without a brain. The entire world of sound and color would display itself before him, but he would be helpless in it.

At this stage of his esoteric development the student realizes, through personal inward experience, all that had previously appealed to his sense of truth, to his intellect and reason. He has now direct knowledge of his higher self. He learns how his higher self is connected with exalted spiritual beings and forms with them a united whole. He sees how the lower self originates in a higher world, and it is revealed to him how his higher nature outlasts his lower. He can now distinguish the imperishable in himself from the perishable; that is, he learns through personal insight to understand the doctrine of the incarnation of the higher self in the lower. It will become plain to him that he is part of a great spiritual complex, and that his qualities and destiny are due to this connection. He learns to recognize the law of his life, his *karma*. He realizes that his lower self, constituting his present existence, is only one of the forms which his higher being can adopt. He discerns the possibility of working down from his higher self in his lower self, so that he may perfect himself ever more and more. Now, too, he can comprehend the great differences between human beings in regard to their level of perfection. He becomes aware that there are others above him who have already traversed the stages which still lie before him, and he realizes that the teachings and deeds of such men

186

proceed from the inspiration of a higher world. He owes this knowledge to his first personal glimpse into this higher world. The so-called initiates of humanity now become vested with reality for him.

These, then, are the gifts which the student owes to his development at this stage: insight into his higher self; insight into the doctrine of the incarnation of this higher being in a lower; insight into the laws by which life in the physical world is regulated according to its spiritual connections, that is, the law of karma; and finally, insight into the existence of the great initiates.

Thus it is said of a student who has reached this stage, that all doubt has vanished from him. His former faith, based on reason and sound thought, is now replaced by knowledge and insight which nothing can undermine. The various religions have presented, in their ceremonies, sacraments, and rites, externally visible pictures of the higher spiritual beings and events. None but those who have not penetrated to the depths of the great religions can fail to recognize this fact. Personal insight into spiritual reality explains the great significance of these externally

187

visible cults. Religious service, then, becomes for the seer an image of his own communion with the higher, spiritual world.

It has been shown how the student, by attaining this stage, becomes in truth a new being. He can now mature to still higher faculties and, by means of the life-currents of his etheric body, control the higher and actual life-element, thus attaining a high degree of independence from the restrictions of the physical body.

VII

THE TRANSFORMATION
OF DREAM LIFE

AN INTIMATION that the student has
reached or will soon reach the stage of development described in the preceding chapter will
be found in the change which comes over his
dream life. His dreams, hitherto confused and
haphazard, now begin to assume a more regular
character. Their pictures begin to succeed each
other in sensible connection, like the thoughts and
ideas of daily life. He can discern in them law,
cause, and effect. The content, too, of his dreams
is changed. While hitherto he discerned only
reminiscences of daily life and transformed impressions of his surroundings or of his physical
condition, there now appear before him pictures
of a world he has hitherto not known. At first
the general character of his dream life remains

unchanged, in as far as dreams are distinguished from waking mental activity by the symbolical presentation of what they wish to express. No attentive observer of dream life can fail to detect this characteristic. For instance, a person may dream that he has caught some horrible creature, and he feels an unpleasant sensation in his hand. He wakes to discover that he is tightly grasping a corner of the blanket. The truth is not presented to the mind, except through the medium of a symbolical image. A man may dream that he is flying from some pursuer and is stricken with fear. On waking, he finds that he has been suffering, during sleep, from palpitations of the heart. Disquieting dreams can also be traced to indigestible food. Occurrences in the immediate vicinity may also reflect themselves symbolically in dreams. The striking of a clock may evoke the picture of a troop of soldiers marching by to the beat of drums. A falling chair may be the occasion of a whole dream drama in which the sound of the fall is reproduced as the report of a gun, and so forth. The more regulated dreams of esoteric students whose etheric body has begun its development retain this symbolical method of expression, but they will cease merely to reflect reality connected with the physical body and physical environment. As the dreams due to the latter causes become more connected, they are mingled with similar pictures expressing things and events of another world. These are the first experiences lying beyond the range of waking consciousness.

Yet no true mystic will ever make his experiences in dreams the basis of any authoritative account of a higher world. Such dreams must be merely considered as providing the first hint of a higher development. Very soon and as a further result, the student's dreams will no longer remain beyond the reach of intellectual guidance as heretofore, but on the contrary, will be mentally controlled and supervised like the impressions and conceptions of waking consciousness. The difference between dream and waking consciousness grows ever smaller. The dreamer remains awake in the fullest sense of the word during his dream life; that is, he is aware of his mastery and control over his own vivid mental activity.

During our dreams we are actually in a world other than that of our senses; but with undeveloped spiritual organs we can form none other than the confused conceptions of it described above. It is only in so far present for us as, for instance, the world of sense could be for a being equipped with no more than rudimentary eyes. That is why we can see nothing in this world but counterfeits and reflections of daily life. The latter are perceptible to us because our own soul paints its daily experiences in pictorial form into the substance of which that other world consists. It must be clearly understood that in addition to our ordinary conscious work-a-day life we lead a second, unconscious life in that other world. We engrave in it all our thoughts and perceptions. These tracings only become visible when the lotus flowers are developed. Now, in every human being there are slender rudiments of these lotus flowers. We cannot perceive by means of them during waking consciousness because the impressions made on them are very faint. We cannot see the stars during the daytime for a similar reason: their visibility is extinguished by the mighty glare of the sun. Thus, too, the faint spiritual impressions cannot make themselves felt in the face

192

of the powerful impressions received through the senses.

Now, when the gate of the senses is closed during sleep, these other impressions begin to emerge confusedly, and the dreamer becomes aware of experiences in another world. But as already explained, these experiences consist at first merely of pictures engraved in the spiritual world by our mental activity attached to the physical senses. Only developed lotus flowers make it possible for manifestations not derived from the physical world to be imprinted in the same way. And then the etheric body, when developed, brings full knowledge concerning these engraved impressions derived from other worlds.

This is the beginning of life and activity in a new world, and at this point esoteric training must set the student a twofold task. To begin with, he must learn to take stock of everything he observes in his dreams, exactly as though he were awake. Then, if successful in this, he is led to make the same observations during ordinary waking consciousness. He will so train his attention and receptivity for these spiritual impressions that they need no longer vanish in the face of the physical impressions, but will always be at hand for him and reach him in addition to the others.

When the student has acquired this faculty there arises before his spiritual eyes something of the picture described in the preceding chapter, and he can henceforth discern all that the spiritual world contains as the cause of the physical world. Above all things he can perceive and gain knowledge of his own higher self in this world. The next task now confronting him is to grow, as it were, into this higher self, that is, really to regard it as his own true self and to act accordingly. He realizes ever more clearly and intensely that his physical body and what he hitherto called his "I" are merely the instruments of his higher self. He adopts an attitude toward his lower self such as a person limited to the world of the senses adopts toward some instrument or vehicle that serves him. No one includes as part of himself the vehicle in which he is travelling, even though he says: "I travel"; so, too, when an inwardly developed person says: "I go through the door," his actual conception is: "I carry my body

194

through the door." Only this must become a natural concept for him, so that he never for a moment loses his firm footing in the physical world,
or feels estranged from it. If the student is to
avoid becoming a fantastic visionary he must not
impoverish his life through his higher consciousness, but on the contrary, enrich it, as a person
enriches his life by using the railway and not
merely his legs to cover a certain distance.

When the student has thus raised himself to a
life in the higher ego, or rather during his acquisition of the higher consciousness, he will
learn how to stir to life the spiritual perceptive
force in the organ of the heart and control it
through the currents described in the foregoing
chapter. This perceptive force is an element of
higher substantiality, which proceeds from the
organ in question and flows with beautiful radiance through the moving lotus flowers and the
other channels of the developed etheric body.
Thence it radiates outward into the surrounding
spiritual world rendering it spiritually visible, just
as the sunlight falling on the objects of the physical world renders them visible.

How this perceptive force in the heart organ is created can only be gradually understood in the course of actual development.

It is only when this organ of perception can be sent through the etheric body and into the outer world, to illumine the objects there, that the actual spiritual world, as composed of objects and beings, can be clearly perceived. Thus it will be seen that complete consciousness of an object in the spiritual world is only possible when man himself casts upon it the spiritual light. Now, the ego which creates this organ of perception does not dwell within, but outside the physical body, as already shown. The heart organ is only the spot where the individual man kindles, from without, this spiritual light organ. Were the latter kindled elsewhere, the spiritual perceptions produced by it would have no connection with the physical world. But all higher spiritual realities must be related to the physical world, and man himself must act as a channel through which they flow into it. It is precisely through the heart organ that the higher ego governs the physical self, making it into its instrument.

Now, the feelings of an esoterically developed

196

person toward the things of the spiritual world are very different from the feelings of the undeveloped person toward the things of the physical world. The latter feels himself to be at a particular place in the world of sense, and the surrounding objects to be external to him. The spiritually developed person feels himself to be united with, and as though in the interior of, the spiritual objects he perceives. He wanders, in fact, from place to place in spiritual space, and is therefore called the *wanderer* in the language of occult science. He has no home at first. Should he, however, remain a mere wanderer he would be unable to define any object in spiritual space. Just as objects and places in physical space are defined from a fixed point of departure, this, too, must be the case in the other world. He must seek out some place, thoroughly investigate it, and take spiritual possession of it. In this place he must establish his spiritual home and relate everything else to it. In physical life, too, a person sees everything in terms of his physical home. Natives of Berlin and Paris will involuntarily describe London in a different way. And yet there is a difference between the spiritual and the physical home. We are born into the latter without our co-operation and instinctively absorb, during our childhood, a number of ideas by which everything is henceforth involuntarily colored. The student, however, himself founds his own spiritual home in full consciousness. His judgment, therefore, based on this spiritual home, is formed in the light of freedom. This founding of a spiritual home is called in the language of occult science *the building of the hut*.

Spiritual vision at this stage extends to the spiritual counterparts of the physical world, so far as these exist in the so-called astral world. There everything is found which in its nature is similar to human instincts, feelings, desires, and passions. For powers related to all these human characteristics are associated with all physical objects. A crystal, for instance, is cast in its form by powers which, seen from a higher standpoint, appear as an active human impulse. Similar forces drive the sap through the capillaries of the plant, cause the blossoms to unfold and the seed vessels to burst. To developed spiritual organs of perception all these forces appear gifted with form and color, just as the objects of the physical world have form and color for physical eyes. At this

198

stage in his development the student sees not only the crystal and the plant, but also the spiritual forces mentioned above. Animal and human impulses are perceptible to him not only through their physical manifestation in the individual, but directly as objects; he perceives them just as he perceives tables and chairs in the physical world. The whole range of instincts, impulses, desires, and passions, both of an animal and of a human being, constitute the astral cloud or aura in which the being is enveloped.

Furthermore, the clairvoyant can at this stage perceive things which are almost or entirely withheld from the senses. He can, for instance, tell the astral difference between a room full of low or of high-minded people. Not only the physical but also the spiritual atmosphere of a hospital differs from that of a ballroom. A commercial town has a different astral air from that of a university town. In the initial stages of clairvoyance this perceptive faculty is but slightly developed; its relation to the objects in question is similar to the relation of dream consciousness to waking consciousness in ordinary life; it will, however, become fully awakened at this stage as well.

The highest achievement of a clairvoyant who has attained the degree of vision described above is that in which the astral counter-effects of animal and human impulses and passions are revealed to him. A loving action is accompanied by quite a different astral concomitant from one inspired by hate. Senseless desire gives rise to an ugly astral counterpart, while a feeling evoked by a high ideal creates one that is beautiful. These astral images are but faintly perceptible during physical life, for their strength is diminished by life in the physical world. The desire for an object, for example, produces a counterpart of this sort in addition to the semblance of the desire itself in the astral world. If, however, the object be attained and the desire satisfied, or if, at any rate, the possibility of satisfaction is forthcoming, the corresponding image will show but faintly. It only attains its full force after the death of the individual human being, when the soul in accordance with her nature still harbors such desires, but can no longer satisfy them, because the object and the physical organ are both lacking. The gourmand, for instance, will still retain, after death, the desire to please his palate; but there is no possibility of satisfying this desire because he no longer has a palate. As a result, the desire produces an especially powerful counterpart, by which the soul is tormented. These experiences evoked by the counterparts of the lower soul-nature after death are called the experiences in the soul-world, especially in the region of desires. They only vanish when the soul has purified herself from all desires inclining toward the physical world. Then only does the soul mount to the higher regions, to the world of spirit. Even though these images are faint during life in the physical world, they are none the less present, following man as his world of desire, in the way a comet is followed by its tail. They can be seen by a clairvoyant at the requisite stage of development.

Such and similar experiences fill the life of the student during the period described above. He cannot attain higher spiritual experience at this stage of development, but must climb still higher from this point.

VIII

THE CONTINUITY OF CONSCIOUSNESS

UMAN life runs its course in three alternating states or conditions, namely, waking, dreaming sleep, and dreamless sleep. The attainment of the higher knowledge of spiritual worlds can be readily understood if a conception be formed of the changes occurring in these three conditions, as experienced by one seeking such higher knowledge. When no training has been undertaken to attain this knowledge, human consciousness is continually interrupted by the restful intervals of sleep. During these intervals the soul knows nothing of the outer world, and equally little of itself. Only at certain periods dreams emerge from the deep ocean of insensibility, dreams linked to the occurrences of the outer world or the conditions of the physical body. At

202

first, dreams are only regarded as a particular manifestation of sleep-life, and thus only two states are generally spoken of, namely, sleeping and waking. For spiritual science, however, dreams have an independent significance apart from the other two conditions. In the foregoing chapter a description was given of the alteration ensuing in the dream-life of the person undertaking the ascent to higher knowledge. His dreams lose their meaningless, irregular and disconnected character and form themselves more and more into a world of law and order. With continued development, not only does this new world born out of the dream world come to be in no way inferior to outer physical reality as regards its inner truth, but facts reveal themselves in it representing a higher reality in the fullest sense of the word. Secrets and riddles lie concealed everywhere in the physical world. In the latter, the effects are seen of certain higher facts, but no one can penetrate to the causes whose perception is confined merely to his senses. These causes are partly revealed to the student in the condition described above and developed out of dream life, a condition, however, in which he by no means remains stationary. True, he must not regard these revelations as actual knowledge so long as the same things do not also reveal themselves during ordinary waking life. But in time he achieves this as well: he develops this faculty of carrying over into waking consciousness the condition he created for himself out of dream life. Thus something new is introduced into the world of his senses that enriches it. Just as a person born blind and successfully operated upon will recognize the surrounding objects as enriched by all that the eye perceives, so, too, will anyone having become clairvoyant in the above manner perceive the whole world surrounding him peopled with new qualities, things, beings, and so forth. He now need no longer wait for his dreams to live in another world, but he can at any suitable moment put himself into the above condition for the purpose of higher perception. This condition then acquires a significance for him similar to the perception, in ordinary life, of things with active senses as opposed to inactive senses. It can truly be said that the student opens the eyes of his soul and beholds things which necessarily remain concealed from the bodily senses.

Now, this condition is only transitional to still higher stages of knowledge. If the student continues his esoteric exercises he will find, in due time, that the radical change, as described above, does not confine itself to his dream life, but that this transformation also extends to what was previously a condition of deep dreamless sleep. Isolated conscious experiences begin to interrupt the complete insensibility of this deep sleep. Perceptions previously unknown to him emerge from the pervading darkness of sleep. It is, of course, not easy to describe these perceptions, for our language is only adapted to the physical world, and therefore only approximate terms can be found to express what does not at all belong to that world. Still, such terms must be used to describe the higher worlds, and this is only possible by the free use of simile; yet seeing that everything in the world is interrelated, the attempt may be made. The things and beings of the higher worlds are closely enough related to those of the physical world to enable, with a little good will, some sort of conception of these higher worlds to be formed, even though words suitable for the physical world are used. Only the reader must always bear in mind that such descriptions of supersensible worlds must, to a large extent, be in the nature of simile and symbol. The words of ordinary language are only partially adopted in the course of esoteric training; for the rest, the student learns another symbolical language, as a natural outcome of his ascent to higher worlds. The knowledge of this language is acquired during esoteric training itself, but that does not preclude the possibility of learning something concerning the higher worlds even from such ordinary descriptions as those here given.

Some idea can be given of those experiences which emerge from the insensibility of deep sleep if they be compared to a kind of hearing. We may speak of perceptible tones and words. While the experiences during dreaming sleep may fitly be designated as a kind of vision, the facts observed during deep sleep may be compared to auricular impressions. (It should be remarked in passing that for the spiritual world, too, the faculty of sight remains the higher. There, too, colors are higher than sounds and words. The student's first perceptions in this world do not yet extend to the higher colors, but only to the lower tones. Only because man, according to his general development, is already more qualified for the world revealing itself in dreaming sleep does he at once perceive colors there. He is less qualified for the higher world unveiling itself in deep sleep; therefore the first revelations of it he receives are in tones and words; later on, he can here, too, ascend to colors and forms.)

Now, when these experiences during deep sleep first come to the notice of the student, his next task must be to sense them as clearly and vividly as possible. At first this presents great difficulty, the perception of these experiences being exceedingly slight. The student knows very well, on waking, that he has had an experience, but is completely in the dark as regards its nature. The most important thing during this initial stage is to remain quiet and composed, and not for a moment lapse into any unrest or impatience. The latter is under all circumstances detrimental; it can never accelerate development, but only delays it. The student must cultivate a quiet and yielding receptivity for the gift that is presented to him; all violence must be repressed. Should he at any period not become aware of experiences during sleep he must wait patiently until this is possible. Some day this moment will assuredly arrive. And this perceptive faculty, if awaited with patience and composure, remains a secure possession; while should it appear momentarily in answer to forcible methods, it may be completely lost for a long time.

Once this perceptive faculty is acquired and the experiences during sleep are present to the student's consciousness in complete lucidity and clarity, his attention should be directed to the following point. All these experiences are seen to consist of two kinds, which can be clearly distinguished. The first kind will be totally different from anything that he has ever experienced. These experiences may be a source of joy and edification, but otherwise they should be left to themselves for the time being. They are the first harbinger of higher spiritual worlds in which the student will find his way later on. In the other kind of experiences the attentive observer will discover a certain relationship with the ordinary world in which he lives. The subjects of his reflections during life, what he would like to understand in these things around him but cannot understand with the ordinary intellect, these are the things concerning which the experiences during sleep give him information. During every-day life man reflects on his environment; his mind tries to conceive and understand the connection existing between things; he seeks to grasp in thought and idea what his senses perceive. It is to these ideas and concepts that the experiences during sleep refer. Obscure, shadowy concepts become sonorous and living in a way comparable only to the tones and the words of the physical world. It seems to the student ever more and more as though the solution of the riddles over which he ponders is whispered to him in tones and words out of a higher world. And he is able to connect with ordinary life whatever comes to him from a higher world. What was formerly only accessible to his thought now becomes actual experience, just as living and substantial as an experience in this physical world can be. The things and beings of this physical world are by no means only what they appear to be for physical perception. They are the expression and effluence of a spiritual world.

This spiritual world, hitherto concealed from the student, now resounds for him out of his whole environment.

It is easy to see that this higher perceptive faculty can prove a blessing only if the opened soul-senses are in perfect order, just as the ordinary senses can only be used for a true observation of the world if their equipment is regular and normal. Now man himself forms these higher senses through the exercises indicated by spiritual science. The latter include concentration, in which the attention is directed to certain definite ideas and concepts connected with the secrets of the universe; and meditation, which is a life in such ideas, a complete submersion in them, in the right way. By concentration and meditation the student works upon his soul and develops within it the soul-organs of perception. While thus applying himself to the task of concentration and meditation his soul grows within his body, just as the embryo child grows in the body of the mother. When the isolated experiences during sleep begin, as described, the moment of birth is approaching for the liberated soul; for she has literally become a new being, developed by the individual within

210

himself, from seed to fruit. The effort required for concentration and meditation must therefore be carefully and accurately maintained, for it contains the laws governing the germination and fruition of the higher human soul-being. The latter must appear at its birth as a harmonious, well-proportioned organism. Through an error in following the instructions, no such normal being will come to existence in the spiritual spheres, but a miscarriage incapable of life.

That this higher soul-being should be born during deep sleep will be easily grasped, for if that delicate organism lacking all power of resistance chanced to appear during physical every-day life it could not prevail against the harsh and powerful processes of this life. Its activity would be of no account against that of the body. During sleep, however, when the body rests in as far as its activity is dependent on sense perception, the activity of the higher soul, at first so delicate and inconspicuous, can come into evidence. Here again the student must bear in mind that these experiences during sleep may not be regarded as fully valid knowledge, so long as he is not in a position to carry over his awakened higher soul into waking consciousness as well. The acquisition of this faculty will enable him to perceive the spiritual world in its own character, among and within the experiences of the day; that is, the hidden secrets of his environment will be conveyed to his soul as tones and words.

Now, the student must realize at this stage of development that he is dealing with separate and more or less isolated spiritual experiences. He should therefore beware of constructing out of them a complete whole or even a connected system of knowledge. In this case, all manner of fantastic ideas and conceptions would be mixed into the soul-world, and a world might thus easily be constructed which had nothing to do with the real spiritual world. The student must continually practice self-control. The right thing to do is to strive for an ever clearer conception of the isolated real experiences, and to await the spontaneous arrival of new experiences which will connect themselves, as though of their own accord, with those already recorded. By virtue of the power of the spiritual world into which he has now found his way, and through continued application to the prescribed exercises, the student experiences an ever increasing extension and expansion of consciousness during sleep. The unconscious intervals during sleep-life grow ever smaller, while more and more experiences emerge from erstwhile unconsciousness. These experiences thus link themselves together increasingly of their own accord, without this true unity being disturbed by all manner of combinations and inferences, which in any case would only originate in an intellect accustomed to the physical world. Yet the less the habits of thought acquired in the physical world are allowed to play into these higher experiences, the better it is.

By thus conducting himself the student approaches ever nearer to the attainment of that condition, on his path to higher knowledge, in which the unconsciousness of sleep-life is transformed into complete consciousness. When his body rests, man lives in surroundings which are just as real as those of his waking daily life. It is needless to say that the reality during sleep is different from physical reality surrounding the physical body. The student learns—indeed he must learn if he is to retain a firm footing in the physical world and not become a visionary—to connect the higher experiences of sleep with his physical environment. At first, however, the world entered during sleep is a completely new revelation. This important stage of development, at which consciousness is retained in the life during sleep, is known in spiritual science as the *continuity of consciousness*. The condition here indicated is regarded, at a certain stage of development, as a kind of ideal, attainable at the end of a long path. What the student first learns is the extension of consciousness into two soul-states, in the first of which only disordered dreams were previously possible, and in the second only unconscious dreamless sleep. Anyone having reached this stage of development does not cease experiencing and learning during those intervals when the physical body rests, and when the soul receives no impressions through the instrumentality of the senses.

IX

THE SPLITTING OF THE HUMAN PER-
SONALITY DURING SPIRITUAL
TRAINING

DURING sleep no impressions are conveyed
to the human soul through the instrumentality of the physical sense-organs. The impressions from the ordinary outer world do not find
their way to the soul when in that condition. In
certain respects the soul is actually outside that
part of the human being—the so-called physical
body—which in waking life is the medium for
sense perceptions and thought. The soul is then
only connected with the finer bodies (the etheric
body and the astral body), which are beyond the
scope of physical sense observation. But the
activity of these finer bodies does not cease during
sleep. Just as the physical body is connected and
lives with the things and beings of the physical
world, affecting them and being affected by them,

215

so, too, does the soul live in a higher world; only, this life of the soul continues also during sleep. The soul is in full activity during sleep, but we can know nothing of this activity so long as we have no spiritual organs of perception through which to observe what is going on around us and see what we ourselves are doing during sleep, as we observe our daily physical environment with our ordinary senses. The preceding chapters have shown that esoteric training consists in the development of such spiritual sense organs. Now if, as a result of esoteric training, the student's life during sleep is transformed in the manner described in the foregoing chapter, he will, when in that condition, be able to follow consciously everything going on around him. He can at will find his way in his environment as he could, when awake, with his ordinary senses. It should here be noted that a higher degree of clairvoyance is required for the higher perception of ordinary physical environment. This was indicated in the last chapter. In the initial stages of his development the student perceives things pertaining to another world without being able to discern their connection with the objects of his daily physical environment.

These characteristics of life during sleep or in dreams illustrate what is continually taking place in the human being. The soul lives in uninterrupted activity in the higher worlds, ever gathering from them the impulse to act upon the physical body. Ordinarily unconscious of his higher life, the esoteric student renders himself conscious of it, and thereby his whole life becomes transformed. As long as the soul remains unseeing in the higher sense it is guided by superior cosmic beings. And just as the life of a person born blind is changed, through a successful operation, from its previous dependence on a guide, so too is the life of a person changed through esoteric training. He outgrows the principle of being guided by a master and must henceforward undertake to be his own guide. The moment this occurs he is, of course, liable to commit errors totally unknown to ordinary consciousness. He acts now from a world from which, formerly, higher powers unknown to him influenced him. These higher powers are directed by the universal cosmic har-

217

mony. The student withdraws from this cosmic harmony, and must now himself accomplish things which were hitherto done for him without his co-operation.

It is for this reason that so much is found in books dealing with these matters concerning the dangers connected with the ascent into higher worlds. The descriptions sometimes given of these dangers may well make timid souls shudder at the prospect of this higher life. Yet the fact is that dangers only arise when the necessary precautions are neglected. If all the measures counselled by true esoteric science are adopted, the ascent will indeed ensue through experiences surpassing in power and magnitude everything the boldest flights of sense-bound fantasy can picture; and yet there can be no question of injury to health or life. The student meets with horrible powers threatening life at every turn and from every side. It will even be possible for him to make use of certain forces and beings existing beyond physical perception, and the temptation is great to control these forces for the furtherance of personal and forbidden interests, or to employ them wrongly out of a deficient knowledge of the higher worlds. Some of these especially important experiences, for instance the meeting with the Guardian of the Threshold, will be described in the following chapters. Yet we must realize that the hostile powers are none the less present, even though we know nothing of them. It is true that in this case their relation to man is ordained by higher powers, and that this relation alters when the human being consciously enters this world hitherto concealed from him. But at the same time his own existence is enhanced and the circle of his life enriched by a great and new field of experience. A real danger can only arise if the student, through impatience or arrogance, assumes too early a certain independence with regard to the experiences of the higher worlds; if he cannot wait to gain really sufficient insight into the supersensible laws. In these spheres, modesty and humility are far less empty words than in ordinary life. If the student possesses these qualities in the very best sense he may be certain that his ascent into the higher life will be achieved without danger to all that is commonly called health and life. Above all things, no disharmony must ensue between the higher experiences and the events and demands of every-day life. Man's task must be entirely

219

sought for on this earth, and anyone desiring to shirk his earthly task and to escape into another world may be certain he will never reach his goal. Yet what the senses perceive is only part of the world, and it is in the spirit world that the beings dwell who express themselves in the facts of the physical world. Man must become a partaker of the spirit in order to carry its revelations into the physical world. He transforms the earth by implanting in it what he has ascertained in the spiritual world. That is his task. It is only because the physical world is dependent upon the spiritual, and because man can work upon earth, in a true sense, only if he is a participator in those worlds in which the creative forces lie concealed—only for these reasons should he have the desire to ascend to the higher worlds. No one approaching esoteric training with these sentiments, and resolved not to deviate for a moment from these prescribed directions, need fear the slightest danger. No one should allow the prospect of these dangers to deter him from esoteric training; it should rather act as a strong challenge to one and all to acquire those faculties which every true esoteric student must possess.

After these preliminary observations that should dispel any element of terror, a description of some of the so-called dangers will be given. It is true that great changes take place in the student's finer bodies, as described above. These changes are connected with certain processes in the development of the three fundamental forces of the soul, with willing, feeling, and thinking. Before esoteric training, these forces are subject to a connection ordained by higher cosmic laws. Man's willing, feeling, and thinking are not arbitrary. A particular idea arising in the mind is attended by a particular feeling, according to natural laws; or it is followed by a resolution of the will in equally natural sequence. We enter a room, find it stuffy, and open the window. We hear our name called and follow the call. We are questioned and we answer. We perceive an ill-smelling object and experience a feeling of disgust. These are simple connections between thinking, feeling, and willing. When we survey human life we find that everything is built up on such connections. Indeed, life is not termed normal unless such a connection, founded on the laws of human nature, is observed between thinking, feel-

ing, and willing. It would be found contrary
to these laws if the sight of an ill-smelling object
gave anyone pleasure, or if anyone, on being questioned, did not answer. The success anticipated
from a right education or fitting instruction is
based upon the presumption that a connection between thinking, feeling, and willing, corresponding to human nature, can be established in the pupil. Certain ideas are conveyed to him on the as-
sumption that they will be associated, in regular
fashion, with his feelings and volitions.

All this arises from the fact that in the finer
soul-vehicles of man the central points of the three
forces—thinking, feeling, and willing—are connected with each other according to laws. This
connection in the finer soul organism has its
counterpart in the coarser physical body. In the
latter, too, the organs of will are connected
according to laws with those of thinking and feeling. A particular thought, therefore, inevitably
evokes a feeling or an activity of will. In the
course of higher development, the threads inter-
connecting the three fundamental forces are
severed. At first this severance occurs only within
the finer soul organism, but at a still higher stage

the separation extends also to the physical body. It is a fact that in higher spiritual development the brain divides into three separate parts. This separation is not physically perceptible in the ordinary way, nor can it be demonstrated by the keenest instruments. Yet it occurs, and the clairvoyant has means of observing it. The brain of the higher clairvoyant divides into three independently active entities: the thought-brain, the feeling-brain, and the will-brain.

Thus the organs of thinking, feeling, and willing become individualized; their connection henceforth is not maintained by laws inherent in themselves, but must be managed by the awakened higher consciousness of the individual. This, then, is the change which the student observes coming over him: that no connection arises of itself between an idea and a feeling or a will-impulse, unless he himself provides one. No impulse urges him from thought to action unless he himself in freedom gives rise to this impulse. He can henceforth confront, devoid of feeling, a fact which before his training would have filled him with glowing love or bitter hatred; and he can remain impassive at a thought which formerly

223

would have spurred him on to action, as though of its own accord. He can perform actions through resolutions of the will for which there is not the slightest reason for anyone not having undergone esoteric training. The student's great achievement is the attainment of complete mastery over the combined activity of the three soul forces; but at the same time the responsibility for this activity is placed entirely in his own hands.

It is only through this transformation of his being that the student can enter consciously into relation with certain supersensible forces and beings, for his own soul forces are related to certain fundamental forces of the world. The force, for instance, inherent in the will can affect definite things and beings of the higher worlds, and also perceive them; but it can only do so when liberated from its connection with thinking and feeling within the soul. The moment this connection is severed, the activity of the will can be exteriorized. The same applies to the forces of thinking and feeling. A feeling of hatred sent out by a person is visible to the clairvoyant as a fine luminous cloud of special coloring; and the clairvoyant can ward off this feeling of hatred, just as an ordi-

224

nary person wards off a physical blow that is aimed at him. In the supersensible world, hatred becomes a visible phenomenon, but the clairvoyant can only perceive it in so far as he is able to project outwards the force lying in his feeling, just as the ordinary person directs outwards the receptive faculty of his eye. And what is said of hatred applies also to far more important phenomena of the physical world. The student can enter into conscious intercourse with them, thanks to the liberation of the fundamental forces of his soul.

Through the separation of the forces of thinking, feeling, and willing, the possibility of a threefold aberration arises for anyone neglecting the injunctions given by esoteric science. Such an aberration can occur if the connecting threads are severed before the higher consciousness is sufficiently advanced to hold the reins and guide properly the separated forces into free and harmoniously combined activity. For as a rule, the three human soul-forces are not equally advanced in their development at any given period of life. In one person, thinking is ahead of feeling and willing; in a second, another soul-force has the upper hand over its companions. As long as the connection between the soul-forces is maintained as established by higher cosmic laws, no injurious irregularity, in a higher sense, can occur through the predominance of one force or another. Predominating will, for instance, is prevented by the levelling influence of thinking and feeling from lapsing into any particular excesses. When, however, a person of such predominating will undertakes esoteric training, feeling and thinking cease to exert their regular influence on the will when the latter constantly presses on to great exertions of power. If, then, such a person is not sufficiently advanced to control completely the higher consciousness and himself restore harmony, the will pursues its own unbridled way, continually overpowering its possessor. Feeling and thought lapse into complete impotence; the individual is scourged by his over-mastering will. A violent nature is the result, rushing from one unbridled action to another.

A second deviation occurs when feeling unduly shakes off its proper control. A person inclined to the revering of others may then diverge into unlimited dependence, to the extent of losing all personal will and thought. Instead of higher knowl-

226

edge, the most pitiful vacuity and feebleness would become such a person's lot. Or, in the case of such inordinate predominance of the feeling life, a person with an inclination toward religious devotion can sink into the most degenerate welter.

The third evil is found when thought predominates, resulting in a contemplative nature hostile to life and locked up within itself. The world, for such people, has no further importance save that it provides them with objects for satisfying their boundless thirst for wisdom. No thought ever moves them to an action or a feeling. They appear everywhere as cold and unfeeling creatures. They flee from every contact with the things of ordinary life as though from something exciting their aversion, or which, at any rate, had lost all meaning for them.

These are the three ways of error into which the student can stray: (1) exuberant violence of will, (2) sentimental emotionalism, and (3) cold, loveless striving for wisdom. For outward observation, and also from the ordinary (materialistic) medical standpoint, anyone thus gone astray is hardly distinguishable (especially in degree) from an insane or, at least, a highly neurasthenic person. Of course the student must not resemble these. It is essential for him that the three fundamental soul-forces, thinking, feeling, and willing, should have undergone harmonious development before being released from their inherent connection and subordinated to the awakened higher consciousness. For once a mistake is made and one of the soul-forces falls a prey to unbridled excess, the higher soul comes into existence as a miscarriage. The unrestrained force pervades the individual's entire personality, and for a long time there can be no question of the balance being restored. What appears to be a harmless characteristic as long as its possessor is without esoteric training, namely, a predominance of thinking or feeling or willing, is so intensified in an esoteric student that the universally human element, indispensable for life, becomes obscured.

Yet a really serious danger cannot threaten the student until he has acquired the ability to include in his waking consciousness the experiences forthcoming during sleep. As long as there is only the question of illumination of the intervals of sleep, the life of the senses, regulated by universal cosmic laws, reacts during the waking hours on the disturbed equilibrium of the soul, tending to restore the balance. That is why it is so essential that the waking life of the student should be in every respect regular and healthy. The more capable he is of meeting the demands made by the outer world upon a healthy, sound constitution of body, soul, and spirit, the better it is for him. On the other hand, it may be very bad for him if his ordinary waking life affects him in an exciting or irritating way, that is, if destructive or hampering influences of outer life affect him in addition to the great changes taking place in his inner self. He must seek to find everything corresponding to his powers and faculties which can lead him into undisturbed, harmonious communion with his surroundings, while avoiding everything detrimental to this harmony—everything that brings unrest and feverish haste into his life. And here it is not so much a question of casting off this unrest and haste in an external sense, but much more of taking care that thoughts, feelings, intentions, and bodily health are not thereby exposed to continual fluctuation. All this is not so easy for the student to accomplish as it was before esoteric training, for the higher experiences now playing into

his life act upon his entire existence. Should anything within these higher experiences not be as it
should, the irregularity continues lying in wait
for him and may at every turn throw him off the
right path. For this reason the student should
omit nothing which can secure for him unfailing
mastery over his whole being. He should never
be found wanting in presence of mind or in calm
penetration of all situations of life. In the main, a
genuine esoteric training gives rise of itself to all
these qualities, and as it progresses the student
only becomes acquainted with the dangers while
simultaneously and at the right moment acquiring the full power to rout them from the field.

X

THE GUARDIAN OF THE THRESHOLD

THE important experiences marking the student's ascent into the higher worlds include his meeting with the *Guardian of the Threshold*. Strictly speaking, there are two *Guardians:* a *lesser* and a *greater*. The student meets the lesser Guardian when the threads connecting willing, feeling, and thinking within the finer astral and etheric bodies begin to loosen, in the way described in the foregoing chapter. The greater Guardian is encountered when this sundering of the connections extends to the physical parts of the body, that is, at first to the brain. The lesser Guardian is a sovereign being. He does not come into existence, as far as the student is concerned, until the latter has reached the requisite stage of

231

development. Only some of his most important characteristics can here be indicated.

The attempt will now be made to describe in narrative form this meeting with the lesser Guardian of the Threshold, as a result of which the student learns that his thinking, feeling, and willing have become released within him from their inherent connection.

A truly terrible spectral being confronts him, and he will need all the presence of mind and faith in the security of his path which he has had ample opportunity to acquire in the course of his previous training.

The Guardian proclaims his signification somewhat in the following words: "Hitherto, powers invisible to thyself watched over thee. They saw to it that in the course of thy lives each of thy good deeds brought its reward, and each of thine evil deeds was attended by its evil results. Thanks to their influence thy character formed itself out of thy life-experiences and thy thoughts. They were the instruments of thy destiny. They ordained the measure of joy and pain allotted to thee in thine incarnations, according to thy conduct in lives gone by. They ruled over thee as the all-embrac-

232

ing law of *karma*. These powers will now partly release thee from their constraining influence; and henceforth must thou accomplish for thyself a part of the work which hitherto they performed for thee. Destiny struck thee many a hard blow in the past. Thou knewest not why. Each blow was the consequence of a harmful deed in a bygone life. Thou foundest joy and gladness, and thou didst take them as they came. They, too, were the fruits of former deeds. Thy character shows many a beautiful side, and many an ugly flaw. Thou hast thyself to thank for both, for they are the result of thy previous experiences and thoughts. These were till now unknown to thee; their effects alone were made manifest. The karmic powers, however, beheld all thy deeds in former lives, and all thy most secret thoughts and feelings, and determined accordingly thy present self and thy present mode of life. But now all the good and evil sides of thy bygone lives shall be revealed to thee. Hitherto they were interwoven with thine own being; they were in thee and thou couldst not see them, even as thou canst not behold thine own brain with physical eyes. But now they become released from thee; they detach themselves from thy personality. They assume an independent form which thou canst see even as thou beholdest the stones and plants of the outer world. And . . . I am that very being who shaped my body out of thy good and evil achievements. My spectral form is woven out of thine own life's record. Till now thou hast borne me invisibly within thee, and it was well that this was so; for the wisdom of thy destiny, though concealed from thee, could thus work within thee, so that the hideous stains on my form should be blotted out. Now that I have come forth from within thee, that concealed wisdom, too, has departed from thee. It will pay no further heed to thee; it will leave the work in thy hands alone. I must become a perfect and glorious being, or fall a prey to corruption; and should this occur I would drag thee also down with me into a dark and corrupt world. If thou wouldst avoid this, then thine own wisdom must become great enough to undertake the task of that other, concealed wisdom, which has departed from thee. As a form visible to thyself I will never for an instant leave thy side, once thou hast crossed my Threshold. And in future, whenever thou dost act or think wrongly thou wilt straightway perceive thy guilt

234

as a hideous, demoniacal distortion of my form. Only when thou hast made good all thy bygone wrongs and hast so purified thyself that all further evil is, for thee, a thing impossible, only then will my being have become transformed into radiant beauty. Then, too, shall I again become united with thee for the welfare of thy future activity.

"Yet my Threshold is fashioned out of all the timidity that remains in thee, out of all the dread of the strength needed to take full responsibility for all thy thoughts and actions. As long as there remains in thee a trace of fear of becoming thyself the guide of thine own destiny, just so long will this Threshold lack what still remains to be built into it. And as long as a single stone is found missing, just so long must thou remain standing as though transfixed; or else stumble. Seek not, then, to cross this Threshold until thou dost feel thyself entirely free from fear and ready for the highest responsibility. Hitherto I only emerged from thy personality when death recalled thee from an earthly life; but even then my form was veiled from thee. Only the powers of destiny who watched over thee beheld me and could thus, in the intervals between death and a new birth, build in thee, in accordance with my appearance, that power and capacity thanks to which thou couldst labor in a new earth life at the beautifying of my form, for thy welfare and progress. It was I, too, whose imperfection ever and again constrained the powers of destiny to lead thee back to a new incarnation upon earth. I was present at the hour of thy death, and it was on my account that the Lords of Karma ordained thy reincarnation. And it is only by thus unconsciously transforming me to complete perfection in ever recurring earthly lives that thou couldst have escaped the powers of death and passed over into immortality united with me.

"Visible do I thus stand before thee today, just as I have ever stood invisible beside thee in the hour of death. When thou shalt have crossed my Threshold, thou wilt enter those realms to which thou hast hitherto only had access after physical death. Thou dost now enter them with full knowledge, and henceforth as thou wanderest outwardly visible upon the earth thou wilt at the same time wander in the kingdom of death, that is, in the kingdom of life eternal. I am indeed the Angel of Death; but I am at the same time the bearer of a higher life without end. Through me thou wilt die with thy body still living, to be reborn into an imperishable existence.

"Into this kingdom thou art now entering; thou wilt meet beings that are supersensible, and happiness will be thy lot. But I myself must provide thy first acquaintance with that world, and I am thine own creation. Formerly I drew my life from thine; but now thou hast awakened me to a separate existence so that I stand before thee as the visible gauge of thy future deeds—perhaps, too, as thy constant reproach. Thou hast formed me, but by so doing thou hast undertaken, as thy duty, to transform me."

(It will be gathered from the above that the Guardian of the Threshold is an (astral) figure, revealing itself to the student's awakened higher sight; and it is to this supersensible encounter that spiritual science conducts him. It is a lower magical process to make the Guardian of the Threshold physically visible also. That was attained by producing a cloud of fine substance, a kind of frankincense resulting from a particular mixture of a number of substances. The developed power of the magician is then able to mould the frankin-

237

cense into shape, animating it with the still un-redeemed karma of the individual. Such physical phenomena are no longer necessary for those sufficiently prepared for the higher sight; and besides this, anyone who sees, without adequate preparation, his unredeemed karma appear before his eyes as a living creature would run the risk of straying into evil byways. Bulwer Lytton's *Zanoni* contains in novel form a description of the Guardian of the Threshold.)

What is here indicated in narrative form must not be understood in the sense of an allegory, but as an experience of the highest possible reality befalling the esoteric student.

The Guardian must warn him not to go a step further unless he feels in himself the strength to fulfill the demands made in the above speech. However horrible the form assumed by the Guardian, it is only the effect of the student's own past life, his own character risen out of him into independent existence. This awakening is brought about by the separation of will, thought, and feeling. To feel for the first time that one has oneself called a spiritual being into existence is in itself an experience of the deepest significance. The stu-

238

dent's preparation must aim at enabling him to endure the terrible sight without a trace of timidity and, at the moment of the meeting, to feel his strength so increased that he can undertake fully conscious the responsibility for transforming and beautifying the Guardian.

If successful, this meeting with the Guardian results in the student's next physical death being an entirely different event from death as he knew it formerly. He experiences death consciously by laying aside the physical body as one discards a garment that is worn out or perhaps rendered useless through a sudden rent. Thus his physical death is of special importance only for those living with him, whose perception is still restricted to the world of the senses. For them the student dies; but for himself nothing of importance is changed in his whole environment. The entire supersensible world stood open to him before his death, and it is this same world that now confronts him after death.

The Guardian of the Threshold is also connected with other matters. The person belongs to a family, a nation, a race; his activity in this world depends upon his belonging to some such community. His individual character is also connected with it. The conscious activity of individual persons by no means exhausts everything to be reckoned with in a family, a nation, or a race. Besides their character, families, nations, and races have also their destiny. For persons restricted to their senses these things remain mere general ideas; and the materialistic thinker, in his prejudice, will look down with contempt on the spiritual scientist when he hears that for him, family and national character, lineal or racial destiny, are vested in beings just as real as the personality in which the character and destiny of the individual man are vested. The spiritual scientist becomes acquainted with higher worlds of which the separate personalities are members, just as arms and legs are members of the human being. Besides the separate individuals, a very real family and national group soul and racial spirit is at work in the life of a family, a people, or a race. Indeed, in a certain sense the separate individuals are merely the executive organs of these family group souls, racial spirits, and so on. It is nothing but the truth to say, for instance, that a national group soul makes use of each individual man belonging to that nation for the execution of some work. The

240

group soul of a people does not descend into physical reality but dwells in higher worlds and, in order to work in the physical world, makes use of the physical organs of each individual human being. In a higher sense, it is like an architect making use of workmen for executing the details of a building. In the truest sense, everyone receives his allotted task from his family, national, or racial group soul. Now, the ordinary person is by no means initiated into the higher design of his work. He joins unconsciously in the tasks of his people and of his race. From the moment the student meets the Guardian, he must not only know his own tasks, but must knowingly collaborate in those of his folk, his race. Every extension of his horizon necessarily enlarges the scope of his duties. What actually happens is that the student adds a new body to his finer soul-body. He puts on a second garment. Hitherto he found his way through the world with the coverings enveloping his personality; and what he had to accomplish for his community, his nation, his race, was directed by higher spirits who made use of his personality.

And now, a further revelation made to him by the Guardian of the Threshold is that henceforth these spirits will withdraw their guiding hand from him. He must step out of the circle of his community. Yet as an isolated personality he would become hardened in himself and decline into ruin, did he not, himself, acquire those powers which are vested in the national and racial spirits. Many, no doubt, will say: "Oh, I have entirely freed myself from all lineal and racial connections; I only want to be a human being and nothing but a human being." To these one must reply: "Who, then, brought you to this freedom? Was it not your family who placed you in the world where you now stand? Have you not your lineage, your nation, your race to thank for being what you are? They have brought you up; and if now, exalted above all prejudices, you are one of the light-bringers and benefactors of your stock and even of your race, it is to their up-bringing that you owe it. Yes, even when you say you are 'nothing but a human being,' even the fact that you have become such a personality you owe to the spirits of your communities." Only the esoteric student learns what it means to be entirely cut off from his family, national, or racial spirit. He alone realizes, through personal experience, the insignificance of all such education in respect

242

of the life now confronting him. For everything inculcated by education completely melts away when the threads binding will, thought, and feeling are severed. He looks back on the result of all his previous education as he might on a house crumbling away brick by brick, which he must now rebuild in a new form. And again, it is more than a mere symbolical expression to say that when the Guardian has enunciated his first statement, there arises from the spot where he stands a whirlwind which extinguishes all those spiritual lights that have hitherto illumined the pathway of his life. Utter darkness, relieved only by the rays issuing from the Guardian himself, unfolds before the student. And out of this darkness resounds the Guardian's further admonition: "Step not across my Threshold until thou dost clearly realize that thou wilt thyself illumine the darkness ahead of thee; take not a single step forward until thou art positive that thou hast sufficient oil in thine own lamp. The lamps of the guides whom thou hast hitherto followed will now no longer be available to thee." At these words, the student must turn and glance backward. The Guardian of the Threshold now draws aside a veil which till now had concealed deep life-mysteries. The family, national,

243

and racial spirits are revealed to the student in their full activity, so that he perceives clearly on the one hand, how he has hitherto been led, and no less clearly on the other hand, that he will henceforward no longer enjoy this guidance. That is the second warning received at the Threshold from its Guardian.

Without preparation, no one could endure the sight of what has here been indicated. But the higher training which makes it possible at all for the student to advance up to the Threshold simultaneously puts him in a position to find the necessary strength at the right moment. Indeed, the training can be so harmonious in its nature that the entry into the higher life is relieved of everything of an agitating or tumultuous character. His experience at the Threshold will then be attended by a premonition of that felicity which is to provide the keynote of his newly awakened life. The feeling of a new freedom will outweigh all other feelings; and attended by this feeling, his new duties and responsibilities will appear as something which man, at a particular stage of life, must needs take upon himself.

244

XI

LIFE AND DEATH
THE GREATER GUARDIAN OF THE
THRESHOLD

IT HAS been described in the foregoing chapter how significant for the human being is his meeting with the so-called lesser Guardian of the Threshold by virtue of the fact that he becomes aware of confronting a supersensible being whom he has himself brought into existence, and whose body consists of the hitherto invisible results of the student's own actions, feelings, and thoughts. These unseen forces have become the cause of his destiny and his character, and he realizes how he himself founded the present in the past. He can understand why his inner self, now standing to a certain extent revealed before him, includes particular inclinations and habits, and he can also recognize the origin of certain blows of fate that have befallen him. He perceives why he

245

loves one thing and hates another; why one thing makes him happy and another unhappy. Visible life is explained by the invisible causes. The essential facts of life, too—health and illness, birth and death—unveil themselves before his gaze. He observes how before his birth he wove the causes which necessarily led to his return into life. Henceforth he knows that being within himself which is fashioned with all its imperfections in the visible world, and which can only be brought to its final perfection in this same visible world. For in no other world is an opportunity given to build up and complete this being. Moreover, he recognizes that death cannot sever him forever from this world; for he says to himself: "Once I came into this world because, being what I was, I needed the life it provided to acquire qualities unattainable in any other world. And I must remain bound to this world until I have developed within myself everything that can here be gained. I shall some day become a useful collaborator in another world only by acquiring all the requisite faculties in this physical world."

Thanks to his insight into the supersensible world, the initiate gains a better knowledge and appreciation of the true value of visible nature than was possible before his higher training; and this may be counted among his most important experiences. Anyone not possessing this insight and perhaps therefore imagining the supersensible regions to be infinitely more valuable, is likely to underestimate the physical world. Yet the possessor of this insight knows that without experience in visible reality he would be totally powerless in that other invisible reality. Before he can live in the latter he must have the requisite faculties and instruments which can only be acquired in the visible world. Consciousness in the invisible world is not possible without spiritual sight, but this power of vision in the higher world is gradually developed through experience in the lower. No one can be born in the spiritual world with spiritual eyes without having first developed them in the physical world, any more than a child could be born with physical eyes, had they not already been formed within the mother's womb.

From this standpoint it will also be readily understood why the Threshold to the supersensible world is watched over by a Guardian. In no case may real insight into those regions be permitted to anyone lacking the requisite faculties; therefore, when at the hour of death anyone enters the other world while still incompetent to work in it, the higher experiences are shrouded from him until he is fit to behold them.

When the student enters the supersensible world, life acquires quite a new meaning for him; he discerns in the physical world the seed-ground of a higher world, so that in a certain sense the higher will appear defective without the lower. Two outlooks are opened before him; the first into the past and the second into the future. His vision extends to a past in which this physical world was not yet existent; for he has long since discarded the prejudice that the supersensible world was developed out of the sense-world. He knows that the former existed first, and that out of it everything physical was evolved. He sees that he himself belonged to a supersensible world before coming for the first time into this sense-world. But this pristine supersensible world needed to pass through the sense-world, for without this passage its further evolution would not have been possible. It can only pursue its course when certain beings will have developed requisite faculties within the realm of the senses. These beings are none other than human beings. They owe their present life to an imperfect stage of spiritual existence and are being led, even within this stage, to that perfection which will make them fit for further work in the higher world. At this point the outlook is directed into the future. A higher stage of the supersensible world is discerned which will contain the fruits matured in the sense-world. The sense-world as such will be overcome, but its results will be embodied in a higher world.

The existence of disease and death in the sense-world is thus explained. Death merely expresses the fact that the original supersensible world reached a point beyond which it could not progress by itself. Universal death must needs have overtaken it, had it not received a fresh life-impulse. Thus this new life has evolved into a battle with universal death. From the remnants of a dying, rigid world there sprouted the seeds of a new one. That is why we have death and life in the world. The decaying portion of the old world adheres to the new life blossoming from it, and the process of evolution moves slowly. This comes to expression most clearly in man himself. The sheath he bears is gathered from the preserved remnants of the old world, and within this sheath the germ of that being is matured which will live in the future.

Thus man is twofold: mortal and immortal. The mortal is in its last, the immortal in its first stage. But it is only within this twofold world, which finds its expression in the sense-world, that he can acquire the requisite faculties to lead the world to immortality. Indeed, his task is precisely to gather the fruits of the mortal for the immortal. And as he glances at himself as the result of his own work in the past he cannot but say: "I have in me the elements of a decaying world. They are at work in me, and I can only break their power little by little, thanks to the new immortal elements coming to life within me." This is the path leading man from death to life. Could he but speak to himself with full consciousness at the hour of his death, he would say: "The perishing world was my task-master. I am now dying as the result of the entire past in which I am enmeshed. Yet the soil of mortal life has matured the seeds of immortal life. I carry them with me into another world.

If it had merely depended on the past, I could never have been born. The life of the past came to an end with birth. Life in the sense-world is wrested from universal death by the newly formed life-germ. The time between birth and death is merely an expression for the sum of values wrested from the dying past by the new life; and illness is nothing but the continued effect of the dying portions of the past."

In the above the answer will be found to the question why man works his way only gradually through error and imperfection to the good and true. His actions, feelings, and thoughts are at first dominated by the perishing and the mortal. The latter gave rise to his sense-organs. For this reason, these organs and all things activating them are doomed to perish. The imperishable will not be found in the instincts, impulses, and passions, or in the organs belonging to them, but only in the work produced by these organs. Man must extract from the perishable everything that can be extracted, and this work alone will enable him to discard the background out of which he has grown, and which finds its expression in the physical sense-world.

251

Thus the first Guardian confronts man as the counterpart of his two-fold nature in which perishable and imperishable are blended; and it stands clearly proved how far removed he still is from attaining that sublime luminous figure which may again dwell in the pure, spiritual world. The extent to which he is entangled in the physical sense-world is exposed to the student's view. The presence of instincts, impulses, desires, egotistical wishes and all forms of selfishness, and so forth, expresses itself in this entanglement, as it does further in his membership in a race, a nation, and so forth; for peoples and races are but steps leading to pure humanity. A race or a nation stands so much the higher, the more perfectly its members express the pure, ideal human type, the further they have worked their way from the physical and perishable to the supersensible and imperishable. The evolution of man through the incarnations in ever higher national and racial forms is thus a process of liberation. Man must finally appear in harmonious perfection. In a similar way, the pilgrimage through ever purer forms of morality and religion is a perfecting process;

for every moral stage retains the passion for the perishable beside the seeds of an ideal future.

Now, in the Guardian of the Threshold as described above, the product of the past is manifest, containing only so many seeds of the future as could be planted in the course of time. Yet everything that can be extracted from the sense-world must be carried into the supersensible world. Were man to bring with him only what had been woven into his counterpart out of the past, his earthly task would remain but partially accomplished. For this reason the lesser Guardian of the Threshold is joined, after a time, by the greater Guardian. The meeting with the second Guardian will again be described in narrative form.

When the student has recognized all the elements from which he must liberate himself, his way is barred by a sublime luminous being whose beauty is difficult to describe in the words of human language. This encounter takes place when the sundering of the organs of thinking, feeling, and willing extends to the physical body, so that their reciprocal connection is no longer regulated by themselves but by the higher consciousness, which has now entirely liberated itself from physical conditions. The organs of thinking, feeling, and willing will then be controlled from supersensible regions as instruments in the power of the human soul. The latter, thus liberated from all physical bonds, is now confronted by the second Guardian of the Threshold who speaks as follows:

"Thou hast released thyself from the world of the senses. Thou hast won the right to become a citizen of the supersensible world, whence thine activity can now be directed. For thine own sake, thou dost no longer require thy physical body in its present form. If thine intention were merely to acquire the faculties necessary for life in the supersensible world, thou needest no longer return to the sense-world. But now behold me. See how sublimely I tower above all that thou hast made of thyself thus far. Thou hast attained thy present degree of perfection thanks to the faculties thou wert able to develop in the sense-world as long as thou wert still confined to it. But now a new era is to begin, in which thy liberated powers must be applied to further work in the world of the senses. Hitherto thou hast sought only thine own release, but now, having thyself become free, thou canst go forth as a liberator of thy fellows. Until today thou hast striven as an individual, but now seek to coordinate thyself with the whole, so that thou mayst bring into the supersensible world not thyself alone, but all things else existing in the world of the senses. Thou wilt some day be able to unite with me, but I cannot be blessed so long as others remain unredeemed. As a separate freed being, thou wouldst fain enter at once the kingdom of the supersensible; yet thou wouldst be forced to look down on the still unredeemed beings in the physical world, having sundered thy destiny from theirs, although thou and they are inseparably united. Ye all did perforce descend into the sense-world to gather powers needed for a higher world. To separate thyself from thy fellows would mean to abuse those very powers which thou couldst not have developed save in their company. Thou couldst not have descended had they not done so; and without them the powers needed for supersensible existence would fail thee. Thou must now share with thy fellows the powers which, together with them, thou didst acquire. I shall therefore bar thine entry into the higher regions of the supersensible world so long as thou hast not applied

255

all the powers thou hast acquired to the liberation of thy companions. With the powers already at thy disposal thou mayst sojourn in the lower regions of the supersensible world; but I stand before the portal of the higher regions as the Cherub with the fiery sword before Paradise, and I bar thine entrance as long as powers unused in the sense-world still remain in thee. And if thou dost refuse to apply thy powers in this world, others will come who will not refuse; and a higher supersensible world will receive all the fruits of the sense-world, while thou wilt lose from under thy feet the very ground in which thou wert rooted. The purified world will develop above and beyond thee, and thou shalt be excluded from it. Thus thou wouldst tread the *black path,* while the others from whom thou didst sever thyself tread the *white path.*"

With these words the greater Guardian makes his presence known soon after the meeting with the first Guardian has taken place. The initiate knows full well what is in store for him if he yields to the temptation of a premature abode in the supersensible world. An indescribable splendor shines forth from the second Guardian of the

256

Threshold; union with him looms as a far distant ideal before the soul's vision. Yet there is also the certitude that this union will not be possible until all the powers afforded by this world are applied to the task of its liberation and redemption. By fulfilling the demands of the higher light-being the initiate will contribute to the liberation of the human race. He lays his gifts on the sacrificial altar of humanity. Should he prefer his own premature elevation into the supersensible world, the stream of human evolution will flow over and past him. After his liberation he can gain no new powers from the world of the senses; and if he places his work at the world's disposal it will entail his renouncement of any further benefit for himself.

It does not follow that, when called upon to decide, anyone will naturally follow the white path. That depends entirely upon whether he is so far purified at the time of his decision that no trace of self-seeking makes this prospect of felicity appear desirable. For the allurements here are the strongest possible; whereas on the other side no special allurements are evident. Here nothing appeals to his egotism. The gift he receives in the higher regions of the supersensible world is nothing that comes to him, but only something that flows from him, that is, love for the world and for his fellows. Nothing that egotism desires is denied upon the black path, for the latter provides, on the contrary, for the complete gratification of egotism, and will not fail to attract those desiring merely their own felicity, for it is indeed the appropriate path for them. No one therefore should expect the occultists of the white path to give him instruction for the development of his own egotistical self. They do not take the slightest interest in the felicity of the individual man. Each can attain that for himself, and it is not the task of the white occultists to shorten the way; for they are only concerned with the development and liberation of all human beings and all creatures. Their instructions therefore deal only with the development of powers for collaboration in this work. Thus they place selfless devotion and self-sacrifice before all other qualities. They never actually refuse anyone, for even the greatest egotist can purify himself; but no one merely seeking an advantage for himself will ever obtain assistance from the white occultists. Even when they do not refuse their help, he, the seeker, deprives himself of the advantage

258

resulting from their assistance. Anyone, therefore, really following the instructions of the good occultists will, upon crossing the Threshold, understand the demands of the greater Guardian; anyone, however, not following their instructions can never hope to reach the Threshold. Their instructions, if followed, produce good results or no results; for it is no part of their task to lead to egotistical felicity and a mere existence in the supersensible worlds. In fact, it becomes their duty to keep the student away from the supersensible world until he can enter it with the will for selfless collaboration.

APPENDIX

THE path to supersensible knowledge, as described in this book, leads the soul through experiences concerning the nature of which it is especially important to avoid all illusions and misconceptions. Yet it is but natural that the latter should arise in such questions as are here considered. In this connection one of the most serious mistakes occurs when the whole range of inner experience dealt with in true spiritual science is distorted into appearing in the same category as superstition, visionary dreaming, mediumship (spiritism), and other degenerate practices. This distortion is often due to the fact that persons desirous of following the path described in this book are confused with others who in their search for supersensible reality, and as a result of methods foreign to a genuine striving for knowledge, wander into undesirable paths. The experiences through which the human soul lives on the path here described are wholly confined to the realm of psycho-spiritual experience. They are only possible if equal freedom and independence from the bodily life are attained for certain other inner experiences, as is the case during ordinary consciousness, when thoughts are made concerning things outwardly perceived or inwardly felt and willed, thoughts which do not themselves originate in what is perceived, felt, and willed. There are people who deny the existence of such thoughts. They believe that no thought is possible that is not extracted from perceptions or from the inner life dependent on the body. For them, all thoughts are to a certain extent mere reflections of perceptions and of inner experiences. This view, however, can be expressed only by those who have never raised themselves to the faculty of experiencing with their souls a self-sustaining life in pure thought. For others, who have lived through this experience, it is a matter of knowledge that wherever thought dominates the life of the soul to the degree that this thought permeates other soul functions, the human being is involved in an activity in whose origin his body has no share. In the ordinary life of the soul, thought is almost always mixed with other functions: perception, feeling, willing, and so forth. These other functions are effectuated by the body; yet thought plays into them, and to the degree that it does this a process takes place, in and through the human being, in which his body has no share. This can only be denied so long as the illusion is not discarded which arises from observing thought only when the latter is united with other functions. Yet an inner exertion is possible which will enable the thinking part of inner life to be experienced as distinct from everything else. Something consisting in pure thought alone can be detached from the encompassing soul-life, that is, thoughts that are self-sustaining and from which everything provided by perception or bodily conditioned inner life is excluded. Such thoughts reveal themselves through themselves, through what they are, as spiritual supersensible substance. Anyone uniting himself with them, while excluding all perception, all memory, and every other token of inner life, knows himself to be in a supersensible region and experiences himself outside the physical body. For anyone familiar with this whole process, the question can no longer arise: Can the soul live through experiences outside the body in a supersensible world? For it would mean denying what he knows from experience. The only question for him is: What prevents such a positive fact from being recognized? And the answer he finds to this question is that the fact does not reveal itself unless the student first cultivates a condition of soul which allows him to become the recipient of this revelation.

Now, people become at once suspicious when an activity confined entirely to the soul is expected of them, in order that something independent of themselves should reveal itself. They believe that they themselves give the revelation its content because they prepare themselves to receive it. They expect experiences to which they contribute nothing and which allow them to remain quite passive. Should such people, in addition, be ignorant of the simplest scientific requirements for the comprehension of a given fact, they will take for an objective revelation of non-sensible substance contents and productions of the soul in which the soul's conscious participation is reduced be-

263

low the level maintained in sense-perception and will-impelled action. Such are the soul-contents provided by the experiences and revelations of the visionary and the medium. But what comes to the fore through such revelations is not a *supersensible* but a *sub-sensible* world. Human waking life does not run its course completely within the body; the most conscious part of it runs its course on the boundary between the body and the physical outer world; thus the process of perception with the organs of sense is as much an extra-physical process penetrating into the body as a permeation of this process from out the body; so, too, is the life of will, which rests upon the insertion of the human being into the cosmic being, so that what occurs in the human being through his will is simultaneously a link in the chain of cosmic occurrence. In this life of the soul running on the boundary of the physical body, the human being is to a high degree dependent on his physical organization; but the function of thought plays into this activity, and in as much as this is the case, the human being makes himself independent of his bodily organization in the functions of sense perception and willing. In the

264

experiences of the visionary and in mediumistic phenomena the human being becomes completely dependent on his body. He excludes from the life of his soul that function which, in perception and willing, makes him independent of his body. Thus the content and productions of his soul are merely revelations of his bodily life. The experiences of the visionary and the phenomena produced by the medium owe their existence to the fact that a person while thus experiencing and producing is, with his soul, less independent of his body than in ordinary perception and willing. In the experience of the supersensible as indicated in this book, the development of soul-life proceeds in just the opposite direction from that taken by the visionary and the medium. The soul acquires a progressively greater independence of the body than is the case in perceiving and willing. The same independence realized in the experience of pure thought is attained by the soul for a far wider range of activity.

For the supersensible activity of the soul here meant, it is especially important to grasp and realize in the clearest possible way this experience of life in pure thought. For in the main, this experience is already a supersensible activity of the soul, but one in which nothing supersensible is as yet perceived. With pure thought we live in the supersensible; but we experience only *this* in supersensible fashion; we do not yet experience anything else supersensibly. And supersensible experience must be a continuation of that life already attained by the soul when united with pure thought. For this reason it is so important to gain knowledge of this union in the right way, for it is from its comprehension that light shines forth to bring correct insight into the nature of supersensible knowledge. The moment the life of the soul sinks below the level of clear consciousness existing in thought, the soul is on the wrong path as far as true knowledge of the supersensible world is concerned: for the soul is seized by the bodily functions, and what is then experienced is not the revelation of a supersensible world, but bodily revelations confined to the subsensible world.

*   *   *

(2) Having penetrated to the sphere of the supersensible, the soul's experiences are of such a

nature that descriptive expressions cannot so easily be found for them as for experiences confined to the world of the senses. Care must often be taken not to overlook the fact that to a certain extent, in descriptions of supersensible experience, the distance separating the actual fact from the language used to describe it is greater than in descriptions of physical experience. The reader must be at pains to realize that many an expression is intended as an illustration, merely indicating in a delicate way the reality to which it refers. Thus it is said on page 19 of this book: "Originally all rules and teachings of spiritual science were expressed in a symbolical sign-language." And on page 82 a "certain writing system" was mentioned. Now, anyone may easily be led to suppose that such a writing system can be learned in the same way we learn the letters of an ordinary physical language, and their combinations. In this connection it must be pointed out that there have been and there still are spiritual scientific schools and associations possessing symbolical signs by means of which supersensible facts are expressed. And anyone initiated into the meaning of these symbols attains thereby the means of directing his inner life toward the supersensible realities in question. But what is of far greater importance for supersensible experience is that, in the course of that supersensible experience to which the realization of the contents of this book leads, the soul should, in the contemplation of the supersensible, gain the revelation of such a writing through personal experience. The supersensible says something to the soul which the soul must translate into these illustrative signs, so that it can be surveyed with full consciousness. The statement can be made that what is imparted in this book can be realized by every soul. And in the course of this realization, which the soul can personally determine according to the indications given, the resulting events occur as described. Let the reader take this book as a conversation between the author and himself. The statement that the student needs personal instruction should be understood in the sense that this book itself is personal instruction. In earlier times there were reasons for reserving such personal instruction for oral teaching; today we have reached a stage in the evolution of humanity in which spiritual scientific knowledge must become far more widely disseminated than formerly. It must be placed within the reach of everyone to a quite different extent from what was the case in older times. Hence the book replaces the former oral instruction. It is only to a limited extent correct to say that further personal instruction is necessary beyond that contained in this book. No doubt someone may need assistance, and it may be of importance for him or her; but it would be false to believe that there are any cardinal points not mentioned in this book. These can be found by anyone who reads correctly, and, above all, *completely*.

* * *

(3) The descriptive instructions given in this book appear at first sight to require the complete alteration of the whole human being. Yet when correctly read it will be found that nothing more is intended than a description of the inner soul state required of anyone in those moments of life at which he confronts the supersensible world. He develops this state of soul as a second being within himself; and the healthy other being pur-

sues its course in the old way. The unfolding
trainee knows how to hold the two beings apart
in full consciousness and how to make them act
and react on each other in the right way. This
does not make him useless and incompetent for
life, nor does he lose his interest and skill in it
and become a spiritual researcher the whole day
long. It is of course true that the student's manner of experience in the supersensible world will
shed its light over his whole being; but far from
distracting him from life, it makes him more
capable and his life more productive. The
necessity of adopting the existing method of
description is due to the fact that every cognitive
process directed toward the supersensible calls
the whole human being into action; so that in the
moment of such cognition the whole human being is engaged. In the process of color perception
the eye alone with its adjoining nervous system
is engaged, while the supersensible cognitive process engages the whole human being. The whole
human being becomes an eye or an ear. For this
reason, when information is given concerning
the construction of supersensible cognitive processes, it appears as though a transformation of

the human being were meant, as if nothing were right in the ordinary human being, and he should become quite different.

*   *   *

(4) I should like to add to what was said on pp. 131 *et seq.* concerning "some results of initiation," something which, with a slight alteration, can apply to other parts of the book. It may occur to someone to ask whether such figurative descriptions are necessary, and whether it would not be possible to describe these supersensible experiences in ideas, without such illustrations. In reply it must be pointed out that for the experience of supersensible reality it is essential that the human being know himself as a supersensible being in a supersensible world. Without this vision of his own supersensible nature, whose reality is fully manifest in the descriptions here given of the lotus flowers and the etheric body, the human being's experience of himself in the supersensible world would be like placing him in the sensible world in such a way that the things and processes around him manifested themselves, while he himself had no knowledge of his own

271

body. His perception of his own supersensible form in soul-body and etheric body enables him to stand, conscious of himself, in the supersensible world, just as he is conscious of himself in the physical world through the perception of his physical body.

THE END.

BASIC BOOKS

THEOSOPHY, AN INTRODUCTION TO THE SUPER-SENSIBLE KNOWLEDGE OF THE WORLD AND THE DESTINATION OF MAN *by Rudolf Steiner*

In this work Steiner carefully explains many of the basic concepts and terminologies of anthroposophy. The book begins with a sensitive description of the fundamental trichotomy: body, soul, and spirit, elaborating the various higher members of the human constitution. A discussion of reincarnation and karma follows. The next and longest chapter (75 pages) presents, in a vast panorama, the seven regions of the soul world, the seven regions of the land of spirits, and the soul's journey after death through these worlds. A brief discussion of the path to higher knowledge follows.

"Read . . . Rudolf Steiner's little book on theosophy—your hair will stand on end!" Saul Bellow in **Newsweek**

(195 pp)   0-91014-239-4 Paper
                                      0-91014-265-3 Cloth

AN OUTLINE OF OCCULT SCIENCE *by Rudolf Steiner*

This lengthy work begins with a thorough discussion and definition of the term "occult" science. A description of the supersensible nature of the human being follows, along with a discussion of dreams, sleep, death, life between death and rebirth, and reincarnation. In the fourth chapter evolution is described from the perspective of initiation science. The fifth chapter characterizes the training a student must undertake as a preparation for initiation. The sixth and seventh chapters consider the future evolution of the world and more detailed observations regarding supersensible realities.

(188 pp)   0-91014-275-0 Paper
                                      0-91014-226-2 Cloth

CHRISTIANITY AS MYSTICAL FACT *by Rudolf Steiner*

This early fundamental work, written in 1902 enlarged in 1910, seeks to show how Christianity arose out of what was prepared in the pre-Christian Mysteries. Christianity, however, was not merely a further development of what existed in these Mysteries but something unique and independent, arising much in the same way that a seed arises out of the soil. Included are chapters on: The Mysteries and Mystery Wisdom, The Greek Sages Before Plato, Plato as a Mystic, Mystery Wisdom of Egypt, Steiner then goes on to consider: The Gospels, The Lazarus Miracle, The Apocalypse of St. John, Jesus and His Historical Background, The Nature of Christianity, Christianity and Pagan Wisdom, and St. Augustine and the Church. This book is a foundation for what Steiner later more fully develops concerning the nature of Christ and Christianity. Also published in a different translation as *Christianity and Occult Mysteries of Antiquity.*

(195 pp)   0-88010-159-8 Paper

OTHER BOOKS ON
SPIRITUAL DEVELOPMENT

ESOTERIC DEVELOPMENT *by Rudolf Steiner*
These ten lectures and essays given throughout Steiner's life depict the experience of his non-mystical, scientifically clear path to a cultivation of inner faculties for experiencing supersensible realities. Topics covered include the "six basic exercises," fasting, suitable content and practical requirements for meditative training, changes and stages of inner awareness, the role of love in acquiring higher knowledge, the development of higher sense organs or chakras, and the three types of esoteric paths: Oriental Yoga, Christian-Gnostic, and European Rosicrucian.

"With an informative introduction by Alan Howard, Esoteric Development *is a useful introduction to the spiritual development exercises taught by Rudolf Steiner."* **New Age Book Review**

(191 pp)   0-88010-012-5 Paper
                                              0-88010-013-3 Cloth

THE STAGES OF HIGHER KNOWLEDGE *by Rudolf Steiner*
In these four essays Steiner describes the experience of the three higher stages of consciousness: Imagination, Inspiration, and Intuition which are experienced by the student as he progresses on the path to knowledge, and by the initiate. The six exercises for the heart center are characterized as a means of protecting oneself from the "danger of mischief from hurtful forces" which would arise if one practiced meditation without the exercises. This book is a continuation of *Knowledge of Higher Worlds.*

(64 pp)   Paper

THE INNER DEVELOPMENT OF MAN *by Rudolf Steiner*
This is a one-lecture introduction to the nature of esoteric training or path of knowledge. (Berlin, Dec. 15, 1904)

(22 pp.)   Paper

PRACTICAL TRAINING IN THOUGHT *by Rudolf Steiner* (Karlsruhe, 1909)
This most popular pamphlet has been translated into many languages and published in innumerable editions. It is known throughout the world for its clear and concise directions for improving memory, thinking habits and powers of concentration.

(25 pp)   0-910142-29-7 Paper

RUDOLF STEINER AND INITIATION *by Paul Eugen Schiller*
The author is a research scientist and life long student of Steiner's works. In this book, Schiller presents a systematic discussion of Steiner's writings and lectures on the path of knowledge. Among the topics discussed are: "Fundamental Moods," "Development of the Six Attributes," "Sense Free Thinking, Feeling, and Willing," "Meditation," "Body Free Life of the Soul," "The Rosicrucian Path of Initiation," and "The Level of Inspirational Cognition."

(143 pp.)   0-910142-96-3 Paper

WALDORF EDUCATION

The WALDORF or STEINER SCHOOL movement is one of the largest private school systems in the world. There are numerous Steiner schools in the United States with programs from kindergarten through high school. The Anthroposophic Press offers the following titles on this important approach to education:

INTRODUCTION TO WALDORF EDUCATION by *Rudolf Steiner*
A short essay going to the heart of the Waldorf approach. Steiner explains the important changes occurring in the child at the 9th and 12th years and the way the curriculum meets these changes. It is probably the best short introduction to the development philosophy of Waldorf Education available. (This essay is contained in the forthcoming book *Renewal of the Social Organism.*)

(10 pp.)   0-88010-137-7 Booklet

THE EDUCATION OF THE CHILD *by Rudolf Steiner*
This is perhaps the best short introduction to Waldorf education available. It is suitable both for the prospective parent and teacher. The text is an essay revised by Steiner from a lecture of the same title in 1909.

(50 pp.)   0-88010-133-4 Paper

THE RECOVERY OF MAN IN CHILDHOOD *by A.C. Harwood*
Piaget and other modern child development researchers attempt to study the emergence of adult capacities in the child. But, as A.C. Harwood points out in this absorbing study of Rudolf Steiner's educational work, childhood is a time of *losing*, as well as gaining, capacities. Is there a connection between the loss of a childlike faculty and the acquisition of an adult one? Yes, answers Harwood—in fact, a threefold connection.

There follows an insightful survey of the three seven-year stages of child development as depicted by Steiner. This is presented in connection with numerous examples and anecdotes on Waldorf education's use of curriculum subjects to support and assist this developmental child-man exchange. Other chapters take up specific facets of Waldorf education, such as foreign languages, eurythmy and music, and the temperaments. These lucid and literate explanations qualify this book as the most intelligent and stimulating introductory work on that unique approach to educating known often as "education as an art."

(211 pp)   0-88010-001-X Paper

TEACHING AS A LIVELY ART *by Marjorie Spock*
The author systematically describes the stages of a child's development from 6 to 13 years of age. The education methods appropriate to these different periods are discussed. There are also chapters on the temperaments, the teacher, and the relation between teacher and child.

(138 pp)   0-91014-285-5 Paper

ORDERING INFORMATION

All the books described on the preceding pages are available from:

Anthroposophic Press
Bell's Pond, Star Route
Hudson, NY 12534

Free catalog listing hundreds of titles available on request.